CYBER FORENSICS &DIGITAL SECURITY

AI-Driven Cybercrime Investigations and Risk Management

Olakunle Bayode Falana

TABLE OF CONTENTS

DEDICATION

To the cybersecurity professionals, forensic analysts, and digital risk experts who work tirelessly to protect our digital world this book is for you.

To the innovators, researchers, and visionaries pushing the boundaries of cyber forensics and artificial intelligence, your contributions shape the future of digital security.

To every mentor, educator, and leader who has inspired the next generation of cybersecurity experts, your guidance is invaluable.

And to my family, friends, and colleagues who have supported this journey, your encouragement has been my greatest strength.

This book stands as a testament to the relentless pursuit of knowledge, security, and excellence in the face of evolving digital threats.

PREFACE

In an era where cyber threats are becoming increasingly sophisticated, the need for advanced cybersecurity and digital forensics has never been greater. The rapid integration of artificial intelligence in cybercrime, digital risk management, and forensic investigations demands a new level of expertise, precision, and adaptability. This book, Cyber Forensics and Digital Security: AI-Driven Cybercrime Investigations and Risk Management, is designed to provide cybersecurity professionals, forensic analysts, security engineers, and law enforcement agencies with a comprehensive guide to navigating the complexities of modern digital threats.

This work is not just a technical manual; it is a deep dive into the evolving landscape of cybercrime and the role of AI in forensic investigations. It explores cutting-edge methodologies for tracking digital threats, analyzing cyber incidents, and implementing proactive security measures. From penetration testing and forensic evidence analysis to risk mitigation strategies, this book provides real-world insights into combating cyber threats at scale.

The objective of this book is to bridge the gap between theory and practice, offering both foundational knowledge and advanced techniques for tackling digital security challenges. By combining AI-driven forensic methodologies with traditional cybersecurity practices, professionals will be equipped to identify, analyze, and respond to cyber incidents more efficiently. Whether you are a seasoned cybersecurity expert or an aspiring digital forensics specialist, this book serves as a valuable resource in understanding and mastering the intricacies of cyber forensics in today's AI-driven world.

I invite you to explore the pages ahead with an open mind, a keen eye for detail, and a readiness to adopt innovative solutions. Cybersecurity is a field that thrives on continuous learning and adaptation, and this book aims to empower its readers with the necessary tools and knowledge to stay ahead of evolving threats.

Let us embark on this journey into the world of cyber forensics and digital security, where intelligence, technology, and strategic thinking converge to protect and secure the digital world.

FOREWORD

The world of digital security is more complex and critical than ever before. As cyber threats continue to evolve and digital infrastructures grow increasingly sophisticated, the demand for professionals who can navigate this landscape has reached unprecedented heights. Among the key areas of this discipline, cyber forensics and risk management play an essential role in not only responding to incidents but also preventing them.

Olakunle Falana's work in the field of cybersecurity and digital forensics has made him a thought leader whose contributions are shaping the future of the industry. This book, Cyber Forensics and Digital Security: AI-Driven Cybercrime Investigations and Risk Management, is a comprehensive guide that addresses some of the most pressing challenges faced by today's security professionals. It takes readers on a journey through the complex landscape of digital forensics, from investigative methodologies to AI-powered tools that can predict and mitigate cyber threats.

What sets this book apart is its timely exploration of AI in cyber forensics, an area that is rapidly gaining prominence. Olakunle's expertise in integrating AI with traditional forensic techniques offers a glimpse into the future of digital security. His approach not only emphasizes the importance of understanding the technology but also stresses the need for professionals to stay ahead of cybercriminals who are continually adapting to new technologies.

As someone who has worked extensively in this field, I can confidently say that this book will be an invaluable resource for cybersecurity professionals, forensic analysts, and anyone looking to understand the evolving nature of cybercrime.

Olakunle's ability to distill complex topics into actionable insights ensures that readers, whether novices or experts, will find significant value in the book.

In the pages ahead, you will find a thorough exploration of the tools, techniques, and methodologies that are defining the future of digital forensics. It is my hope that this work will inspire a new generation of cybersecurity professionals to continue pushing the boundaries of innovation and excellence in the field.

INTRODUCTION

In an era defined by rapid technological evolution, digital transformation has become both a remarkable catalyst for progress and a complex terrain of risk. As businesses, governments, and individuals increasingly rely on interconnected systems, the threats that accompany this digital integration have grown more sophisticated, persistent, and dangerous. Cybercrime is no longer a peripheral concern; it is now one of the most significant challenges of the digital age, with implications that span privacy, national security, financial integrity, and global trust.

This book, Cyber Forensics and Digital Security: AI-Driven Cybercrime Investigations and Risk Management, emerges from the urgent need to address these growing threats with precision, intelligence, and innovation. It offers a comprehensive exploration of the modern strategies that cybersecurity professionals, forensic analysts, and law enforcement agencies must adopt to keep pace with evolving adversaries. From AI-powered threat detection to the meticulous art of digital evidence analysis, the chapters within this book are designed to provide both foundational knowledge and advanced insights into the ever-expanding world of cyber forensics and risk mitigation.

As you progress through this book, you will encounter real-world case studies, cutting-edge tools, and best practices drawn from years of experience on the digital frontlines. Each chapter is thoughtfully structured to build upon the previous, guiding readers through the intricate layers of cybercrime investigation from initial incident detection to forensic analysis, from vulnerability assessment to enterprise risk management frameworks. Whether you are a seasoned cybersecurity expert or a professional seeking to expand your capabilities, this book offers a roadmap to navigate the complexities of digital crime in an AI-driven world. With each page, we move closer to a more secure, resilient, and intelligent approach to defending the future of our digital lives.

CHAPTER ONE

Introduction to Cyber Forensics and Digital Security

In the rapidly transforming digital landscape, the need for robust cybersecurity measures has become paramount. Cyber forensics and digital security stand as two interwoven disciplines that safeguard critical information, support law enforcement, and ensure the integrity of digital systems. This chapter lays the foundation for understanding the scope, significance, and evolution of cyber forensics and digital security, providing a contextual framework for the rest of the book.

Cyber forensics, often referred to as computer forensics or digital forensics, involves the collection, preservation, analysis, and presentation of digital evidence in a manner that is legally admissible. It plays a critical role in investigating cybercrimes, from data breaches and malware intrusions to intellectual property theft and online fraud. The discipline has grown exponentially in response to the increasing sophistication of cyberattacks and the global reliance on digital systems.

Digital security, on the other hand, encompasses the practices, tools, and policies used to protect information systems against unauthorized access, disruption, or destruction. It involves proactive and reactive strategies to secure data, networks, applications, and devices from cyber threats. As cybercriminals leverage advanced technologies such as artificial intelligence and machine learning, the defense mechanisms must evolve correspondingly.

The intersection of cyber forensics and digital security is crucial. While digital security aims to prevent cyber incidents, cyber forensics focuses on investigating and resolving them. Together, they form a comprehensive approach to managing digital risks. Cyber forensics provides the analytical backbone needed to understand how breaches occur, attribute attacks, and gather evidence for prosecution. Meanwhile, digital security uses this intelligence to build stronger defense frameworks and mitigate future risks.

The significance of these fields extends beyond corporate environments. Governments, law enforcement agencies, financial institutions, healthcare providers, and educational organizations all depend on digital security and cyber forensic capabilities. In recent years, data breaches affecting millions of users have underscored the importance of having a well-prepared incident response and investigation strategy.

Technological advancements have also reshaped the tools and techniques used in cyber forensics and digital security. From forensic imaging and data carving to SIEM (Security Information and Event Management) systems and endpoint detection and response (EDR), professionals now have access to sophisticated resources for both detecting threats and conducting in-depth investigations. Artificial intelligence, in particular, is revolutionizing how analysts process large volumes of data, identify anomalies, and trace digital trails.

Understanding the legal, ethical, and procedural standards in cyber forensics is equally important. Chain of custody, evidence integrity, and compliance with jurisdictional laws are all critical aspects that ensure the admissibility and reliability of digital evidence. Cybersecurity professionals must also navigate issues related to privacy, consent, and international law as digital crimes often transcend national boundaries.

This chapter serves not only as an introduction but also as a call to action for aspiring and seasoned professionals alike. As we delve deeper into the technical, strategic, and operational dimensions of cyber forensics and digital security in subsequent chapters, it becomes clear that a proactive, informed, and ethical approach is essential to defending our digital future.

In a world increasingly shaped by data and connectivity, mastering the fundamentals of cyber forensics and digital security is not just a professional necessity, it is a societal imperative. The chapters that follow will explore the tools, frameworks, methodologies, and real-world applications that define modern cyber forensics, equipping readers with the knowledge needed to investigate cybercrimes, mitigate threats, and contribute to a more secure digital ecosystem.

Understanding the Evolving Cyber Threat Landscape

In the digital age, the nature of threats facing individuals, organizations, and governments has undergone a profound transformation. Traditional crimes have not disappeared, but their digital counterparts have multiplied and grown in complexity. Understanding the evolving cyber threat landscape is crucial for cybersecurity professionals, digital forensic analysts, and anyone charged with the protection of digital infrastructure.

The modern cyber threat environment is characterized by a constant arms race between attackers and defenders. Cybercriminals have become more sophisticated, leveraging advanced technologies, including artificial intelligence (AI), to automate attacks, evade detection, and exploit vulnerabilities in ways previously unimaginable. This chapter explores the dynamics shaping today's threat landscape, with a focus on threat actors, attack vectors, motivations, and the role of emerging technologies.

Threat actors in the current digital landscape are varied and operate with differing motives. They include nation-states, cybercriminal organizations, hacktivists, insiders, and even automated bots. Nation-state actors often engage in cyber espionage, sabotage, and information warfare, using highly coordinated and well-funded operations. Cybercriminal groups pursue financial gain through ransomware, phishing, identity theft, and fraud. Hacktivists, motivated by ideological or political causes, conduct disruptive attacks to promote their agendas. Insider threats, originating from employees or trusted partners, pose a particularly dangerous challenge due to their access to internal systems.

Attack vectors have also expanded significantly. No longer limited to email phishing or malicious downloads, cyber-attacks now exploit cloud services, IoT devices, supply chain weaknesses, mobile platforms, and even deepfake technology. For instance, a supply chain attack may involve inserting malicious code into software before it reaches the end user. IoT vulnerabilities are increasingly exploited due to the sheer number of connected devices and their often-inadequate security configurations. As the attack surface grows, so too does the need for a comprehensive and proactive defense posture.

The motivations behind cyber threats are as diverse as the attackers themselves. Financial profit remains the most common driver, but there are also geopolitical, ideological, and personal motivations. Cyber warfare has become a tool for exerting international pressure, manipulating public opinion, and destabilizing economies. In contrast, some actors are driven by personal grievances, vendettas, or the thrill of the challenge. Understanding these motives is critical for anticipating and mitigating attacks.

Emerging technologies are shaping the future of cyber threats. AI and machine learning are being used not only to defend against cyber-attacks but also to power them. AI-driven malware can adapt to security measures in real time, while deep learning techniques can craft highly convincing social engineering attacks. Likewise, quantum computing, though still in its infancy, poses a potential risk to current cryptographic standards, threatening to render many existing encryption methods obsolete.

To address this dynamic threat environment, organizations must embrace threat intelligence and continuous monitoring. Real-time analysis of threat data, sharing of intelligence across sectors, and the use of AI for predictive analytics are all crucial for maintaining resilience. Cybersecurity is no longer a static set of defenses but a dynamic, intelligence-driven operation that evolves with the threat landscape.

Understanding the evolving cyber threat landscape is not merely an academic exercise, it is a foundational step in building robust digital defenses. As this chapter has illustrated, today's cyber threats are more diverse, more sophisticated, and more persistent than ever before. In the chapters ahead, we will delve deeper into the methods of forensic investigation, AI-driven threat detection, and the development of frameworks designed to combat and manage these ever-changing threats.

The Role of AI in Modern Cybersecurity

Artificial Intelligence (AI) is transforming the cybersecurity landscape into ways that were previously unimaginable. With the rise of increasingly complex cyber threats and the scale at which digital systems operate, traditional approaches to cybersecurity have proven inadequate in many instances. AI offers a revolutionary set of tools and techniques to enhance the detection, analysis, and mitigation of cyber threats in real time. By automating responses, analyzing vast data streams, and adapting to evolving attack patterns, AI is becoming indispensable in the fight against cybercrime.

One of the most significant advantages of AI in cybersecurity is its capacity for predictive analytics. Machine learning algorithms can sift through enormous volumes of data to identify anomalies that may indicate a cyber threat. Unlike static rule-based systems, AI models continuously learn from new data, enabling them to detect novel attack vectors and previously unknown vulnerabilities. This adaptability allows security systems to stay ahead of attackers who are constantly refining their methods to bypass traditional defenses.

AI-driven tools like behavioral analytics, natural language processing, and deep learning algorithms are also enhancing threat intelligence. These tools can parse large datasets from diverse sources network traffic, social media, dark web forums, and threat databases to provide real-time insights into emerging threats. This intelligence is critical for organizations aiming to implement proactive security strategies rather than reactive ones. AI not only identifies threats faster but also classifies them according to risk level, enabling efficient allocation of cybersecurity resources.

In the domain of digital forensics, AI is accelerating the investigation process by automating the identification and extraction of digital evidence. Image recognition tools, speech-to-text converters, and AI-powered forensic platforms can quickly process massive volumes of data, reducing the time investigators spend sifting through files and logs. These capabilities are especially vital in time-sensitive investigations, where every minute counts in preventing further damage or apprehending cybercriminals.

Moreover, AI is streamlining incident response workflows. AI-enabled Security Orchestration, Automation, and Response (SOAR) platforms can autonomously initiate responses to certain types of cyber incidents. For example, if a system detects ransomware activity, AI can isolate the affected network segments, alert administrators, and begin the recovery process within seconds. This rapid response capability reduces the impact of cyber incidents and improves organizational resilience.

However, the integration of AI into cybersecurity also presents challenges. Adversaries are increasingly leveraging AI to craft more sophisticated attacks, such as deepfake technology, AI-generated phishing content, and automated vulnerability discovery. This escalation creates an ongoing arms race where defenders must remain vigilant and continually update their AI defenses. Furthermore, the reliance on AI systems introduces risks related to data integrity, algorithmic bias, and explainability, especially when AI decisions impact legal or regulatory outcomes.

Ethical and governance considerations must also be addressed to ensure AI tools are used responsibly. Ensuring transparency in AI decision-making, maintaining data privacy, and establishing clear accountability for AI-driven actions are essential components of a secure AI cybersecurity framework. These considerations are particularly relevant in sectors like finance, healthcare, and government, where data sensitivity and compliance requirements are paramount.

Despite these challenges, the potential of AI to revolutionize cybersecurity is undeniable. From threat detection and forensic investigation to automated response and predictive defense, AI is enhancing the capabilities of cybersecurity professionals and redefining what is possible in digital protection. As cyber threats continue to evolve, so too, the tools we use to defend against them, and AI stands at the forefront of this digital revolution.

Importance of Cyber Forensics in Digital Investigations

In today's hyper-connected world, digital footprints are left behind with every action taken online whether intentional or not. These footprints serve as vital evidence in cybercrime investigations, making cyber forensics an indispensable part of modern law enforcement, enterprise security, and national defense. Cyber forensics enables investigators to reconstruct cyber incidents, identify perpetrators, and understand the scope of a breach or malicious activity. This investigative discipline not only supports legal proceedings but also strengthens proactive threat detection and mitigation strategies.

At its core, cyber forensics is the scientific process of identifying, preserving, analyzing, and presenting digital evidence. This process involves sophisticated tools and methodologies designed to ensure the integrity and admissibility of data. Whether it's recovering deleted files, analyzing logs, or tracing digital transactions, cyber forensics provides clarity in complex, often opaque cyber incidents. For organizations, the ability to conduct internal digital investigations is not just a technical necessity but a critical component of operational resilience and regulatory compliance.

What elevates the importance of cyber forensics further is its intersection with other branches of cybersecurity such as threat intelligence, penetration testing, and risk management. In the event of a breach, forensic specialists work alongside incident response teams to determine the root cause, identify exploited vulnerabilities, and implement corrective actions. This collaborative approach transforms forensic analysis from a reactive function into a proactive defense strategy, helping prevent future attacks.

Moreover, with the rise of AI-driven threats and deeply obfuscated malware, the scope of digital forensics is expanding rapidly. Analysts are now required to trace not only conventional attack vectors but also complex behavioral anomalies and machine-generated attacks. This demands a combination of technical expertise, analytical thinking, and robust forensic frameworks. As such, the role of cyber forensics has evolved from a niche capability into a cornerstone of digital trust and security assurance.

CHAPTER TWO

Foundations of Cybercrime Investigations

Cybercrime investigations form the backbone of modern digital security efforts. As cyber threats become more sophisticated, understanding the foundational principles of cybercrime investigations is essential for building effective cybersecurity frameworks. This chapter provides an in-depth exploration of the processes, tools, methodologies, and challenges associated with investigating cybercrime. It highlights the importance of a structured investigative approach, the need for digital forensics, and the essential role of cybersecurity professionals in detecting and responding to criminal activities in the digital realm.

The Evolution of Cybercrime Investigations

Cybercrime has evolved dramatically since the advent of the internet and digital technologies. Early cybercrimes were often limited to simple hacking activities, such as unauthorized access to systems or data theft. Over the years, cybercrime has become more diverse and complex, incorporating a range of activities including identity theft, financial fraud, ransomware attacks, data breaches, and cyber terrorism. As these crimes have evolved, so too have the methods for investigating them. Early digital forensics relied on simple techniques like log analysis and keyword searches. However, as cybercriminals adopted more advanced tactics, investigators developed more sophisticated tools and strategies to track and trace digital footprints.

The field of cybercrime investigations has grown to encompass various specializations, each with its own set of challenges and investigative techniques. For instance, financial fraud investigators focus on tracing illicit transactions, while digital forensics experts examine hard drives and cloud storage to uncover evidence of criminal activities. Regardless of the specific type of cybercrime being investigated, the foundational principles of cybercrime investigations remain the same: collecting and preserving evidence, analyzing it in a forensically sound manner, and using it to build a case for prosecution.

Key Principles of Cybercrime Investigations

At the heart of any successful cybercrime investigation is a set of key principles that guide investigators in the proper handling of digital evidence. These principles help ensure the integrity of the investigation, maintain the legal admissibility of evidence, and ensure that suspects' rights are protected. Some of the most important principles include:

- **Chain of Custody**: This refers to the documentation and tracking of evidence from the moment it is collected until it is presented in court. Maintaining a strict chain of custody is crucial for ensuring that evidence has not been tampered with or altered in any way. Every piece of digital evidence must be carefully documented, including its location, who handled it, and when it was collected.

- **Forensic Soundness**: Cybercrime investigations rely heavily on digital evidence, such as hard drives, memory cards, and cloud storage. Investigators must ensure that any evidence collected is preserved in a forensically sound manner, meaning that it is not altered or destroyed during the collection process. This involves using specialized tools and techniques to make copies of digital evidence and preserve the original.

- **Integrity of Evidence**: Once evidence is collected, it must be protected and analyzed in a way that ensures its integrity is maintained. Any tampering with digital evidence whether intentional or accidental can severely undermine an investigation and render the evidence inadmissible in court. Investigators must follow the best practices and established protocols to preserve the integrity of the evidence.

Digital Forensics: Tools and Techniques

Digital forensics is the discipline of recovering, analyzing, and preserving data from digital devices to use as evidence in cybercrime investigations. Digital forensics is central to cybercrime investigations, and its tools and techniques are vital for uncovering valuable evidence. The digital forensics process typically involves the following steps:

- **Identification**: Identifying potential sources of evidence is the first step in a digital forensics' investigation. This includes identifying devices, such as computers, smartphones, and servers, that may contain relevant data. In the case of cloud-based crimes, investigators may need to identify virtual machines, cloud storage accounts, and other online resources.

- **Collection**: Once relevant sources of evidence are identified, the next step is to collect the evidence in a forensically sound manner. This involves creating exact copies (known as images) of hard drives, memory cards, and other digital media. The use of write-blockers ensures that no data is altered during the collection process.

- **Preservation**: Preserving digital evidence is crucial to maintaining its integrity. Investigators must ensure that the collected evidence is securely stored and protected from contamination or tampering. Data must be kept in its original form, without being altered or compromised.

- **Analysis**: Once evidence is collected and preserved, the analysis phase begins. Forensic analysts use specialized tools to examine the collected data for traces of criminal activity. This can include searching for deleted files, examining email communications, analyzing network logs, and performing keyword searches. The analysis process is methodical and thorough, as investigators must identify relevant evidence without damaging or corrupting the data.

- **Presentation**: After the analysis phase, investigators must present their findings in a clear and understandable manner. This often involves generating reports or visual representations of the evidence to help legal professionals and stakeholders understand the results of the investigation. In some cases, investigators may be required to testify in court about their findings.

Types of Cybercrime Investigations

Cybercrime investigations can cover a wide range of criminal activities, each requiring different approaches and expertise. Some of the most common types of cybercrime investigations include:

- **Financial Fraud**: Financial cybercrime often involves illegal activities such as online banking fraud, credit card fraud, and identity theft. Investigators in this field focus on tracing illicit transactions and uncovering the financial schemes behind them. They work closely with financial institutions, credit card companies, and law enforcement agencies to identify and apprehend perpetrators.

- **Hacking and Data Breaches**: Hackers often gain unauthorized access to computer systems, stealing sensitive data or causing damage to networks. Investigators in this area focus on identifying the source of the breach, understanding the methods used by hackers, and preventing further attacks. This type of investigation often involves analyzing logs, network traffic, and system configurations.

- **Ransomware**: Ransomware attacks involve the encryption of a victim's files or systems, followed by a demand for payment in exchange for restoring access. Investigators focus on identifying the ransomware strain, tracing its origins, and gathering evidence to track down the perpetrators. This often involves analyzing ransom notes, examining the behavior of the malware, and identifying payment transactions related to the attack.

- **Child Exploitation and Pornography**: Investigations into cybercrimes involving child exploitation are some of the most sensitive and challenging. Investigators in this field must be highly trained to handle disturbing material, and they work closely with child protection agencies, law enforcement, and other organizations to track down perpetrators and prevent further exploitation.

- **Intellectual Property Theft**: Intellectual property (IP) theft is a growing concern for businesses and organizations. Cybercriminals may steal sensitive company data, such as trade secrets or proprietary software, and use it for financial gain. Investigators focus on tracing stolen intellectual property, identifying the criminals involved, and recovering the stolen assets.

Challenges in Cybercrime Investigations

While cybercrime investigations have advanced significantly over the years, there are still numerous challenges that investigators face. Some of the key challenges include:

- **Anonymity and Encryption**: Cybercriminals often use sophisticated techniques to hide their identities and activities. Anonymity tools, such as Tor and VPNs, allow perpetrators to mask their location and online activities. Additionally, encryption technologies can make it difficult for investigators to access data even if they have seized a device. Overcoming these challenges requires advanced investigative skills and the use of specialized tools.

- **Cross-Jurisdictional Issues**: Cybercrime is a global issue, and investigations often involve multiple jurisdictions. This can make it difficult for investigators to coordinate efforts across borders, particularly when different countries have varying laws and regulations regarding digital forensics and data privacy.

- **Rapid Technological Advancements**: As technology continues to evolve, so too do the methods used by cybercriminals. Investigators must stay up to date with the latest tools and techniques used by criminals, as well as emerging technologies such as artificial intelligence and blockchain. This requires ongoing training and the adoption of new technologies to stay ahead of the curve.

The Role of Cybersecurity Professionals

Cybersecurity professionals play a critical role in cybercrime investigations. From conducting digital forensics to analyzing security logs and preventing data breaches, they are essential for ensuring that organizations remain secure in the face of evolving threats. Their expertise is vital for identifying vulnerabilities, mitigating risks, and investigating incidents when they occur. As the digital world becomes more interconnected, the role of cybersecurity professionals in cybercrime investigations will continue to grow in importance.

The foundations of cybercrime investigations are crucial to building a comprehensive digital security framework. By understanding the key principles, tools, and techniques used in cybercrime investigations, cybersecurity professionals are better equipped to address the challenges posed by modern-day cybercriminals. The field of cybercrime investigation is constantly evolving, but the need for skilled investigators and advanced tools remains essential. As cyber threats become increasingly complex, the role of digital forensics and cybercrime investigations will continue to be pivotal in maintaining cybersecurity and ensuring the safety of individuals and organizations in the digital realm.

A. Cybercrime Categories and Attack Vectors

Cybercrime is a broad and evolving field, with attackers using various techniques to exploit vulnerabilities in digital systems. The increasing sophistication of these attacks demands that cybersecurity professionals stay vigilant and understand the specific categories of cybercrime and the attack vectors through which these crimes occur. This section breaks down the key categories of cybercrime and the different attack vectors that perpetrators use to infiltrate systems, steal sensitive data, and cause harm.

Categories of Cybercrime

Cybercrime can be classified into several distinct categories, each with its own set of characteristics, perpetrators, and targets. Below are some of the most prevalent categories of cybercrime:

1. Hacking and Unauthorized Access: Hacking remains one of the most common forms of cybercrime. Hackers exploit vulnerabilities in systems, networks, and applications to gain unauthorized access to sensitive data. Whether through brute force attacks, exploiting software bugs, or bypassing authentication systems, the goal is often to steal information, disrupt operations, or cause damage. The motivations for hacking can vary: some hackers seek financial gain, others engage in cyber espionage or political activism, while some do it purely for intellectual challenge or notoriety.

Common Techniques Used:

- **SQL Injection**: Malicious code is inserted into SQL queries to exploit vulnerabilities in the database.
- **Brute Force Attacks**: Hackers attempt to guess passwords or encryption keys through trial and error.
- **Credential Stuffing**: Using stolen or leaked credentials to access multiple systems or accounts.

2. Financial Cybercrime: Financial cybercrime involves any illegal activities that impact an individual's or organization's financial assets. This category encompasses a wide range of activities, including online banking fraud, credit card fraud, investment fraud, and the theft of payment card information. Attackers use various methods to siphon money, whether through phishing schemes, skimming devices, or compromising corporate payment systems.

Common Techniques Used:

- **Phishing**: Attackers impersonate legitimate institutions to trick victims into revealing sensitive financial information.

- **Carding**: Fraudulent use of stolen credit card data for unauthorized purchases.

- **Money Laundering**: Using digital platforms or cryptocurrencies to obscure the origins of illicit funds.

3. Intellectual Property Theft: Intellectual property (IP) theft involves the unauthorized use or theft of someone else's creations, such as patents, trademarks, copyrights, or trade secrets. IP theft can occur when cybercriminals steal digital blueprints, software codes, or business strategies. This is particularly prevalent in industries such as technology, pharmaceuticals, and entertainment, where innovative ideas or proprietary information hold substantial value.

Common Techniques Used:

- **Data Breaches**: Cybercriminals steal proprietary business information, including product designs and software code.

- **Reverse Engineering**: Unauthorized deconstruction of software to replicate or steal proprietary technology.

4. Identity Theft: Identity theft occurs when cybercriminals steal personal information such as names, social security numbers, or financial data and use it to impersonate victims for fraudulent purposes. This can lead to a range of crimes, from financial fraud to unlawful access to government services. The theft can be executed via phishing attacks, data breaches, or social engineering techniques.

Common Techniques Used:

- **Social Engineering**: Manipulating individuals to divulge personal information, such as passwords or account numbers.

- **Phishing and Spear Phishing**: Tailored phishing attacks targeting specific individuals to steal sensitive personal information.

5. Cyber Espionage: Cyber espionage refers to the use of hacking to gain access to confidential government or corporate data for political, military, or economic purposes. Nation-state actors or individuals working on their behalf conduct these attacks to gather intelligence, disrupt national security, or gain a competitive advantage. These attacks are often highly sophisticated and may involve espionage tools, custom malware, and long-term infiltration strategies.

Common Techniques Used:

- **Advanced Persistent Threats (APTs)**: A prolonged, targeted cyber-attack aimed at stealing sensitive data from organizations, particularly governmental or military agencies.

- **Zero-Day Exploits**: Attacking vulnerabilities in software that are unknown to the vendor, often used in espionage to gain unauthorized access before a patch is released.

6. Cyberbullying and Online Harassment: Cyberbullying is the use of digital platforms to harass, threaten, or intimidate others. This category includes both personal harassment, such as sending threatening emails or social media messages, as well as the widespread dissemination of malicious content to damage an individual's reputation or cause distress. In extreme cases, cyberbullying can lead to real-world harm or even suicide.

Common Techniques Used:

- **Doxxing**: Publicly revealing private information about an individual to harm their reputation or safety.

- **Trolling and Harassment**: Deliberately provoking or harassing individuals via social media platforms or gaming communities.

Attack Vectors in Cybercrime

An attack vector is a path or method that cybercriminals use to gain unauthorized access to a system or network. Understanding common attack vectors is vital for preventing cybercrime. Below are the primary attack vectors used by cybercriminals:

1. Phishing Attacks: Phishing is one of the oldest and most effective attack vectors. It involves cybercriminals impersonating legitimate organizations, such as banks, social media platforms, or service providers, to trick individuals into divulging sensitive information, such as login credentials, credit card numbers, or personal identification information. Phishing can be conducted through emails, text messages, or phone calls.

Common Techniques:

- **Email Spoofing**: Sending fraudulent emails that appear to come from trusted sources.

- **Spear Phishing**: Targeted phishing attacks aimed at specific individuals or organizations, often involving customized messages.

- **Vishing**: Voice phishing, where attackers call individuals to steal personal information.

2. Malware: Malware is malicious software designed to infect and damage computers, networks, or devices. There are many types of malwares, including viruses, worms, ransomware, and Trojans, each with its own unique capabilities. Malware can be spread through email attachments, infected websites, or software downloads. Once installed on a system, malware can steal data, corrupt files, or even render a device unusable.

Common Types of Malwares:

- **Ransomware**: Encrypts files or locks a system until a ransom is paid to the attacker.
- **Trojans**: Disguised as legitimate software, Trojans allow attackers to gain remote access to a system.
- **Keyloggers**: Software that records keystrokes to capture sensitive information such as passwords.

3. Denial of Service (DoS) and Distributed Denial of Service (DDoS) Attacks: A DoS attack aims to overwhelm a network or server, causing it to become slow or unavailable to legitimate users. In a DDoS attack, multiple compromised systems are used to flood the target with traffic, making it even more difficult to defend against. These attacks can cripple websites, cause financial loss, and damage an organization's reputation.

Common Techniques:

- **Flooding**: Overloading a server with an excessive amount of traffic or data requests.
- **Botnets**: Networks of compromised devices that work together to launch DDoS attacks.

4. Social Engineering: Social engineering attacks rely on psychological manipulation to convince individuals to reveal confidential information or perform actions that compromise security. Attackers exploit human emotions, such as fear, trust, or urgency, to trick victims into falling for scams. Social engineering can be used in combination with other attack vectors, such as phishing, to increase the chances of success.

Common Techniques:

- **Pretexting**: Creating a fabricated story to obtain personal information.
- **Baiting**: Offering something enticing, such as free software or a prize, to lure victims into revealing sensitive information.

5. Exploiting Software Vulnerabilities: Exploiting software vulnerabilities is a common way for attackers to gain unauthorized access to systems. Attackers take advantage of flaws or bugs in operating systems, applications, or network devices. These vulnerabilities can be patched through updates, but if organizations fail to apply security patches, they leave themselves exposed to attack.

Common Techniques:

- **Zero-Day Attacks**: Exploiting vulnerabilities that are unknown to the software vendor and for which no fix is available.
- **SQL Injection**: Inserting malicious SQL code into a web form to manipulate a website's database.

6. Man-in-the-Middle (MitM) Attacks: MitM attacks occur when an attacker intercepts communication between two parties to steal, alter, or manipulate the data being exchanged. This can occur over insecure networks, such as public Wi-Fi, where attackers can intercept sensitive data, including login credentials or credit card information.

Common Techniques:

- **Packet Sniffing**: Monitoring data packets sent across networks to capture sensitive information.
- **Session Hijacking**: Taking over an active session between a user and a service to gain unauthorized access.

Understanding the various categories of cybercrime and the attack vectors used by cybercriminals is essential for building effective cybersecurity defenses. By recognizing the different methods employed by attackers, organizations and individuals can better prepare themselves to defend against these threats. Cybersecurity professionals must stay informed about emerging threats and continuously adapt their security strategies to address new attack vectors and cybercrime categories as they evolve. In an increasingly interconnected world, the importance of understanding cybercrime cannot be overstated, and robust security measures are key to safeguarding digital infrastructures from malicious actors.

B. Legal and Ethical Considerations in Cyber Forensics

In the field of cyber forensics, legal and ethical considerations are paramount. Investigators, cybersecurity professionals, and law enforcement officers must navigate a complex landscape of legal standards, ethical guidelines, and privacy concerns when conducting cybercrime investigations. Failure to adhere to these principles can result in compromised investigations, legal challenges, and significant reputational damage.

The Legal Framework for Cybercrime Investigations

Cyber forensics operates within a legal framework that governs the collection, preservation, and presentation of digital evidence. Different countries and regions have varying laws and regulations regarding cybersecurity, data privacy, and evidence handling. It is crucial for professionals to be familiar with the legal landscape of their jurisdiction to ensure compliance with relevant statutes and avoid legal pitfalls.

Some key legal considerations in cyber forensics include:

- **Data Privacy Laws:** Data privacy laws regulate the collection, processing, and storage of personal information. In many regions, such as the European Union with its General Data Protection Regulation (GDPR), and the United States with the California Consumer Privacy Act (CCPA), data privacy laws are stringent and place a high emphasis on individuals' rights to control their personal data. During a cybercrime investigation, professionals must ensure that they do not violate data privacy laws by collecting or disclosing personal information without proper authorization.

- **Search and Seizure Regulations:** Cyber forensics often requires the search and seizure of digital devices or online data. Law enforcement agencies must follow legal procedures, such as obtaining search warrants, before accessing or seizing electronic evidence. Unauthorized access to systems, such as hacking into an individual's private accounts or systems, can lead to serious legal consequences for investigators. Adhering to search and seizure protocols ensures that evidence is collected legally and remains admissible in court.

- **Chain of Custody:** In the context of cyber forensics, maintaining a proper chain of custody is crucial for ensuring that digital evidence is handled with integrity. The chain of custody refers to the documentation and process that tracks the movement, handling, and storage of evidence from the time it is collected to the point it is presented in court. Any discrepancies in the chain of custody can result in evidence being challenged or deemed inadmissible.

- **International Jurisdictional Issues:** Cybercrime investigations often involve cross-border activities, where the perpetrators may be located in different countries from the victims or evidence. This can create challenges related to jurisdiction and the enforcement of laws across borders. Different countries have different rules for data privacy, evidence handling, and cooperation with foreign law enforcement agencies. Understanding the international legal framework is essential for successful collaboration and the resolution of global cybercrime cases.

Ethical Challenges in Cyber Forensics

Alongside legal considerations, ethical concerns play a vital role in cyber forensics. Investigators must ensure that their actions align with ethical standards, preserving the privacy and rights of individuals while also safeguarding the integrity of the investigation. Below are some ethical considerations that cyber forensics professionals must account for:

- **Maintaining Objectivity and Avoiding Bias:** Cyber forensic investigators must maintain objectivity throughout their work. Biases, whether in favor of the accused or the victim, can distort the investigative process and compromise the outcome. Investigators should approach each case with neutrality and ensure their findings are based solely on the evidence collected, avoiding personal judgments or assumptions.

- **Handling Sensitive Information:** Cyber forensics investigations often involve access to highly sensitive personal data, such as emails, financial records, or private communications. Ethical investigators must handle this information with the utmost confidentiality and ensure it is only used for the purpose of the investigation. Disclosing sensitive information to unauthorized parties or using it for personal gain is a severe breach of ethical standards.

- **Informed Consent:** In some cyber forensics' investigations, particularly those involving online platforms or private data, investigators may need to gain informed consent from individuals or organizations before accessing their information. This is especially important when conducting internal investigations or when the privacy of employees, clients, or third parties is involved. Investigators should always inform stakeholders of their actions and seek consent where necessary, unless legal authority (such as a warrant) permits otherwise.

- **Minimizing Harm:** Cyber forensics professionals should strive to minimize any harm caused during the investigation process. This may involve taking steps to prevent unnecessary exposure of sensitive or personal information, ensuring that data is only accessed when required, and minimizing the impact on individuals' privacy. Ethical considerations also require that investigators avoid actions that could result in undue harm to innocent parties or the wrongful accusation of an individual.

- **Reporting and Transparency:** Transparency is crucial in cyber forensics investigations. Investigators must report their findings accurately and honestly, regardless of the outcome. Falsifying or manipulating evidence is a serious ethical violation and can result in criminal charges. Ethical guidelines also require that investigators clearly document their methods and reasoning throughout the investigation to provide transparency and accountability.

The Importance of Ethical Training in Cyber Forensics

Given the ethical complexities that arise in cyber forensics, it is important for professionals to receive ongoing training in ethical decision-making. Ethical training helps investigators understand how to navigate difficult situations and make sound decisions that comply with legal standards and protect the rights of individuals. Ethical dilemmas may not always have clear-cut answers, so it is essential for cybersecurity professionals to be equipped with the knowledge and tools to handle them appropriately.

Ethical training in cyber forensics should focus on issues such as:

- Understanding the impact of cyber forensics on personal privacy and data protection
- Navigating the ethical challenges of conducting digital investigations in corporate environments
- Adhering to global legal and ethical standards in cross-border cybercrime investigations
- Recognizing potential conflicts of interest and addressing them professionally

By investing in ethical training, organizations and investigators can build trust with stakeholders and ensure the integrity of their forensic work.

Legal and ethical considerations are fundamental to the field of cyber forensics. Cyber forensic investigators must operate within a legal framework that ensures compliance with data privacy laws, proper handling of digital evidence, and adherence to due process. Equally, they must make ethical decisions to ensure that their work does not compromise individuals' privacy or the integrity of the investigation. By understanding and addressing the legal and ethical challenges inherent in cyber forensics, professionals can conduct thorough, reliable, and respectful investigations that serve the interests of justice and security.

C. The Digital Evidence Life Cycle

In the complex world of cyber forensics, one of the most crucial concepts is the Digital Evidence Life Cycle. This life cycle encompasses the stages through which digital evidence passes, from the moment it is collected to its ultimate presentation in court or in a security report. Understanding this life cycle is essential for anyone involved in cybercrime investigations, as it ensures that evidence is handled in a manner that preserves its integrity, reliability, and admissibility.

The Digital Evidence Life Cycle is not merely a linear process but a framework of interconnected stages that form a chain of custody, ensuring that the evidence remains untampered and credible. The integrity of digital evidence is paramount because any breach in this chain can lead to the loss of its legal value. With cybercrimes becoming more sophisticated and increasingly involving complex digital systems, the ability to manage and process digital evidence correctly can be the difference between successfully solving a case or seeing it falter due to mishandling.

Collection: The First Step in Preserving Evidence

The collection stage is the first critical step in the Digital Evidence Life Cycle. Digital evidence can come from a variety of sources, including computers, servers, mobile devices, cloud storage, network traffic, or even social media accounts. During this stage, investigators must use highly specialized techniques and tools to ensure that no data is lost or altered in the process. One of the key aspects of this stage is ensuring that evidence is captured in its original form, preserving its state as it was before being seized. This often involves the use of write blockers, which prevent any changes to the data on the source device, and forensic imaging, which creates an exact copy of the storage media for analysis.

Forensic experts must also ensure that all evidence collected is properly documented, with detailed logs describing the time, place, and method of collection. This documentation becomes vital in court, as it serves as a proof of the chain of custody. If even the smallest discrepancy occurs, the evidence might be challenged as unreliable, and the investigation could fall apart. Additionally, investigators should use proper handling procedures to avoid contamination of the evidence with unrelated data or malware, which could compromise the entire investigation.

Examination: Extracting Meaningful Insights

Once evidence has been collected, the next step in the life cycle is the examination phase. During this stage, forensic analysts begin analyzing the collected data to extract useful information. This involves various techniques such as data carving, keyword searching, timeline analysis, and recovering deleted files or fragments of files that may have been overlooked. Forensic experts often rely on specialized software tools, such as EnCase, FTK (Forensic Toolkit), or Autopsy, to aid in the recovery and analysis of digital evidence.

One of the primary challenges in this phase is sifting through large volumes of data. In today's world, data comes in massive quantities, and it is easy for investigators to become overwhelmed. The key is to apply targeted strategies, using algorithms and advanced search techniques to identify patterns, anomalies, or specific pieces of evidence that can help solve the case. This phase may also involve examining network logs, system event logs, and metadata to understand the scope and impact of a cyber incident, such as a data breach or cyber-attack.

Analysis: Making Sense of the Evidence

Once the relevant data has been identified, it moves to the analysis phase, where forensic analysts interpret the findings. This step is critical, as it transforms raw data into meaningful information that can either prove or disprove a suspect's involvement in a cybercrime. The analysis involves looking at the evidence within its context, considering the methods used by the attacker, the timeline of events, and the broader implications of the findings.

For instance, in the case of a cyber-attack, the analysis might focus on identifying the origin of the attack, the method of intrusion, and the subsequent impact on the targeted organization. Analysts may also examine email metadata to trace communications between suspects, or they might study logs to reconstruct the sequence of actions taken by the attacker. This stage is where expertise in understanding network behavior, system operations, and the tactics employed by cybercriminals becomes invaluable.

Moreover, it is important that forensic experts present their findings in a way that is comprehensible to a variety of stakeholders, including law enforcement agencies, legal teams, or corporate decision-makers. This requires not only technical proficiency but also the ability to communicate complex findings clearly and effectively.

Documentation: Preserving Evidence for Court

The documentation phase is another vital part of the Digital Evidence Life Cycle. Every step taken during the collection, examination, and analysis of digital evidence must be thoroughly documented to ensure that the evidence can be presented in court or to other authorities. The documentation should include detailed reports outlining the methods used, tools involved, the findings, and how the evidence supports or contradicts the case. In many cases, experts will prepare reports that not only describe the data but also provide an interpretation of its meaning and relevance to the investigation.

Documentation also involves maintaining the chain of custody records. These records track the movement of evidence from one handler to another and provide a log of all actions taken during the investigation. In court, any gaps or discrepancies in the chain of custody could render the evidence inadmissible, so meticulous record-keeping is essential. The documentation phase ensures that the evidence is credible and can stand up to scrutiny, whether in court or during an audit.

Presentation: The Final Step in the Life Cycle

The final step in the Digital Evidence Life Cycle is the presentation of the evidence. Whether in court, during an internal investigation, or in a report to an organization's senior leadership, the evidence must be presented clearly, accurately, and persuasively. This presentation often involves preparing visual aids, such as charts, timelines, or network diagrams, that help illustrate the findings in an understandable manner.

Forensic experts must also be ready to testify in court as expert witnesses, explaining the process used to collect, examine, and analyze the evidence. The goal of this phase is not only to present the facts but also to persuade the audience of the validity of the findings. Whether the case results in a conviction, civil penalty, or the resolution of an internal investigation, the way evidence is presented can heavily influence the outcome.

Maintaining Evidence Integrity Throughout the Life Cycle

At every stage of the Digital Evidence Life Cycle, maintaining the integrity of the evidence is paramount. A breach in integrity at any point whether during collection, examination, analysis, documentation, or presentation can undermine the entire case. This is why forensic analysts follow strict protocols and use specialized tools designed to ensure that the evidence is preserved in its original state. Even small deviations, such as accessing evidence without proper authorization or altering files during analysis, can render the entire investigation invalid.

In conclusion, the Digital Evidence Life Cycle is a critical framework in cyber forensics, guiding professionals through each stage of handling digital evidence. From collection to presentation, each step plays a vital role in ensuring that evidence is preserved, analyzed, and presented in a manner that is both accurate and admissible. Forensic professionals must approach each phase with precision, care, and a keen understanding of the legal, technical, and ethical responsibilities involved. As cybercrime continues to evolve, maintaining a firm grasp on this life cycle is essential for staying ahead in the battle to secure digital environments and bring cybercriminals to justice.

CHAPTER THREE

AI and Machine Learning in Cyber Forensics

The increasing complexity and volume of cybercrime have made traditional investigative methods insufficient for modern-day digital security challenges. As organizations and law enforcement agencies face increasingly sophisticated cyber-attacks, there is a growing need for more advanced tools and methodologies in cyber forensics. Artificial Intelligence (AI) and Machine Learning (ML) are now at the forefront of revolutionizing cyber forensic investigations, offering unprecedented capabilities to detect, analyze, and prevent cybercrime.

AI and Machine Learning bring a level of efficiency and precision that was previously unattainable with manual methods. These technologies can analyze vast amounts of data, recognize patterns, and identify anomalies that might otherwise go unnoticed. By automating tedious tasks, AI allows forensic analysts to focus their attention on more complex investigative work, streamlining the entire process and enhancing the accuracy of digital investigations.

The Role of AI in Cyber Forensics

AI in cyber forensics serves as an essential tool for enhancing traditional investigative techniques. One of its most important roles is in automating the process of evidence collection and analysis. In large-scale cybercrime investigations, vast amounts of data are generated from different sources, including servers, cloud storage, and network logs. AI can quickly and efficiently sift through this data to identify potential evidence and areas of interest, significantly reducing the time required for manual analysis.

AI also plays a critical role in the detection of malware and other malicious activities. Machine learning algorithms can be trained to recognize signs of cyber-attacks by analyzing historical data and identifying patterns of behavior that typically precede or accompany an intrusion. These algorithms can learn from past incidents, becoming more adept at detecting evolving threats and unusual activity within networks. Through anomaly detection and predictive modeling, AI-powered systems can flag potential threats and prevent cyber-attacks before they escalate.

Furthermore, AI in cyber forensics is instrumental in analyzing large datasets to identify digital footprints and trace criminal activity. By leveraging AI's advanced search capabilities, investigators can track patterns of communication, pinpoint the origin of cyber-attacks, and establish connections between different data points that might not be immediately apparent. This level of insight is crucial for understanding the full scope of an attack and identifying the individuals or groups responsible.

Machine Learning: Enhancing Forensic Investigations

Machine learning, a subset of AI, is particularly useful in developing models for predicting and detecting cyber threats. Unlike traditional methods that rely on static rules and patterns, machine learning algorithms have the ability to learn and adapt to new and evolving cyber threats. This makes them invaluable in the constantly shifting landscape of cybercrime, where attackers are constantly developing new tactics and methods.

In forensic investigations, machine learning models can be trained on large sets of historical data, allowing them to recognize patterns associated with specific types of cybercrime. For example, machine learning algorithms can be trained to identify patterns of data access, unusual file modifications, or the typical behavior of specific malware types. These models can then be used to detect similar behavior in new datasets, flagging potential security breaches or digital evidence that requires further investigation.

Machine learning can also improve the process of evidence analysis by automating repetitive tasks, such as file classification and categorization. Forensic investigators often face the challenge of analyzing large volumes of data, which can be time-consuming and error-prone when done manually. Machine learning tools can help by automating the identification of important files and evidence, ensuring that investigators can focus their attention on the most relevant data without wasting time on irrelevant or redundant information.

AI and ML in Malware Analysis

One of the most powerful applications of AI and machine learning in cyber forensics is in malware analysis. Cyber-attacks often involve sophisticated malware that can be difficult to detect and analyze. Traditional methods of malware analysis involve manually examining files and processes for signs of malicious activity, a process that can be time-consuming and ineffective against new or unknown malware strains.

With AI and machine learning, however, investigators can take a more proactive approach. Machine learning algorithms can be trained to recognize malicious patterns of behavior and detect malware based on its characteristics rather than relying on known signatures. AI can analyze the behavior of files, applications, and network traffic in real-time to identify potential threats, even if the specific malware has never been seen before. This enables cybersecurity professionals to detect zero-day vulnerabilities and prevent malware attacks before they can cause significant damage.

Machine learning can also assist in reverse engineering malware to understand its structure and behavior. By applying algorithms that analyze the code and behavior of malicious software, forensic analysts can gain insights into how the malware works, how it spreads, and what kind of damage it is designed to inflict. This understanding is critical for developing effective countermeasures and protecting against future attacks.

Predictive Analytics in Cyber Forensics

Another powerful tool that AI and machine learning bring to cyber forensics is predictive analytics. Predictive analytics involves using historical data to predict future events or trends. In cyber forensics, predictive models can help identify potential threats before they occur, allowing organizations to take preemptive action.

For example, AI-powered systems can analyze patterns of network traffic, user behavior, and attack methods to predict when and where an attack is likely to occur. By identifying these patterns, security teams can proactively address vulnerabilities and implement measures to prevent attacks before they happen. Predictive analytics can also help identify the tactics and techniques commonly used by cybercriminals, enabling organizations to better prepare for future threats.

This predictive capability is particularly useful in preventing large-scale cyber-attacks, such as Distributed Denial-of-Service (DDoS) attacks, ransomware, or insider threats. By anticipating potential risks and vulnerabilities, organizations can strengthen their defenses and minimize the damage caused by cybercrime.

Ethical Considerations in AI and ML for Cyber Forensics

While the use of AI and machine learning in cyber forensics offers significant benefits, it also raises important ethical considerations. As these technologies become more integrated into investigative processes, concerns about privacy, data security, and potential misuse arise. For example, AI systems may have access to large volumes of sensitive data, raising questions about how that data is handled and whether it could be used inappropriately.

To address these concerns, it is essential that forensic experts follow strict ethical guidelines and regulatory standards when using AI and machine learning in investigations. Proper oversight, transparency, and accountability must be built into AI systems to ensure they are used responsibly and ethically. Furthermore, cybersecurity professionals must consider the potential for bias in machine learning algorithms, as biased data can lead to inaccurate or unfair outcomes.

It is crucial that AI and machine learning are used in a way that respects individuals' rights and maintains the integrity of the investigation. Ensuring that these technologies are deployed in an ethical and lawful manner will help to foster trust in their effectiveness and encourage their continued use in cyber forensics.

The Future of AI and ML in Cyber Forensics

AI and machine learning are transforming the field of cyber forensics, making it possible to handle the increasing complexity and volume of digital evidence. These technologies enhance the efficiency of investigations, improve the accuracy of threat detection, and enable predictive analytics that helps prevent future cyber-attacks. As cybercrime continues to evolve, the role of AI and machine learning in forensic investigations will become even more important.

Forensic investigators, cybersecurity professionals, and law enforcement agencies must stay at the forefront of these technological advancements to remain effective in the fight against digital crime. By embracing AI and machine learning, they can improve their ability to detect, analyze, and prevent cybercrime, ultimately strengthening the resilience of digital infrastructures and safeguarding critical assets from cyber threats.

A. Leveraging AI for Threat Detection and Analysis

As cyber threats grow in both complexity and scale, organizations are increasingly turning to advanced technologies to stay one step ahead of cybercriminals. One of the most significant technological advancements in the realm of cybersecurity is Artificial Intelligence (AI). AI is revolutionizing how security professionals detect, analyze, and respond to cyber threats. Leveraging AI for threat detection and analysis enables organizations to identify potential risks faster, more accurately, and with greater efficiency, ultimately strengthening their overall cybersecurity posture.

AI systems, particularly machine learning (ML) and deep learning algorithms, have the ability to sift through vast amounts of data at incredible speeds, identifying patterns that may go unnoticed by traditional security tools. By processing information in real-time and continuously adapting to new data, AI can detect anomalies, unusual behaviors, and potential vulnerabilities within a network or system before they manifest as active threats.

Detecting Emerging Threats with AI

One of the most powerful applications of AI in cybersecurity is its ability to detect emerging threats and zero-day vulnerabilities. Traditional security measures often rely on signature-based detection methods, which are only effective against known threats. However, cybercriminals are constantly evolving their tactics, deploying new malware, and finding innovative ways to bypass conventional defenses. AI's ability to recognize anomalous behavior and patterns allows it to detect unknown threats even before a signature has been created or identified.

For instance, AI-driven systems can analyze network traffic, endpoint behavior, and system interactions to identify deviations from normal activity. If, for example, a user suddenly begins accessing large amounts of sensitive data at unusual times, or a system exhibits unexpected behavior, AI can flag these activities for further investigation. By correlating a wide range of data points, AI-powered systems can identify the "footprints" of cyber-attacks, even if they are part of a novel, never-before-seen strategy.

Machine learning models are trained on large datasets, and over time, they learn the normal patterns and behaviors of an organization's network. When unusual activity occurs, the system can raise alerts, providing security teams with critical insights into potential vulnerabilities. AI's ability to detect these abnormalities in real-time is invaluable, enabling security professionals to act swiftly before a cybercriminal can exploit the weaknesses.

Real-Time Threat Detection

A critical advantage of AI in cybersecurity is its ability to conduct real-time threat detection. Unlike traditional methods, which may rely on batch processing or scheduled scans, AI systems continuously monitor network traffic, endpoints, and user behaviors to identify and respond to threats as soon as they emerge. This ability to provide 24/7 vigilance enhances an organization's security infrastructure, allowing for rapid detection and mitigation of attacks such as Distributed Denial-of-Service (DDoS), ransomware, and data exfiltration attempts.

In the case of a DDoS attack, for example, AI-powered systems can quickly detect an increase in traffic to a specific network or server. By analyzing traffic patterns in real-time, AI can distinguish between legitimate user activity and malicious traffic. This quick detection enables security teams to act immediately, mitigating the attack and minimizing damage to critical systems.

Moreover, AI's ability to analyze vast amounts of data in real-time also allows it to identify potential insider threats. If an employee's behavior suddenly deviates from their typical activity, such as accessing systems or data they have no business with, AI can raise a flag and alert security personnel. The earlier an insider threat is detected, the more effectively it can be neutralized.

Automating Threat Response

AI is not only valuable in detecting threats but also in automating responses. Traditional methods of cybersecurity often require manual intervention to respond to potential threats, which can lead to delays and human error. However, AI can automate responses to common threats, providing an immediate, consistent reaction to security incidents. This automation can be crucial in mitigating damage, especially in cases of widespread or fast-moving attacks.

For example, when an AI system detects a malware infection on a device, it can automatically isolate the device from the network to prevent further spread of the malware. Similarly, AI can automatically block malicious IP addresses or revoke access for compromised user accounts, buying valuable time for security teams to investigate and respond.

This automated response reduces the time it takes to contain and remediate cyber threats, which is critical in minimizing potential data loss, financial damage, and reputation harm. It also enables security teams to focus their efforts on more complex issues, such as investigating advanced persistent threats (APTs) or analyzing high-level incidents that require human expertise.

Enhancing Threat Intelligence with AI

AI plays a pivotal role in enhancing threat intelligence, which is essential for understanding and responding to the evolving landscape of cyber threats. Traditional threat intelligence gathering methods often involve sifting through large volumes of data manually, such as network logs, security alerts, and external threat feeds. AI automates this process, aggregating data from a variety of sources internal and external into a unified threat intelligence platform.

By leveraging natural language processing (NLP) and machine learning, AI can analyze and correlate data from various sources, including dark web forums, malware reports, and real-time network activity. This holistic view of the threat landscape allows security teams to better understand the tactics, techniques, and procedures (TTPs) of cybercriminals. Furthermore, AI can predict emerging threats by identifying trends, such as new attack vectors or vulnerabilities being exploited in the wild.

AI-enhanced threat intelligence also improves the accuracy of threat attribution, which is essential for determining the source of an attack. By correlating attack patterns with known adversary profiles, AI can help identify the cybercriminal groups or nation-states behind specific attacks. This level of insight is invaluable for organizations to understand the intent and potential impact of cyber-attacks, as well as to tailor their defense strategies accordingly.

Predictive Analytics and Proactive Defense

One of the most powerful applications of AI in cybersecurity is its ability to predict future threats before they materialize. By analyzing historical attack data, AI systems can identify patterns and trends that suggest where the next threat may originate. This predictive capability allows organizations to be proactive in their defense strategies, shifting from reactive to anticipatory measures.

AI systems use predictive analytics to assess risk factors, such as vulnerabilities within systems, network infrastructure, and employee behavior. For instance, AI can analyze previous attack vectors to identify which systems or applications are most likely to be targeted in future attacks. Based on this analysis, organizations can take preemptive actions, such as patching vulnerable systems, enhancing security controls, and training employees on identifying phishing attempts.

By predicting and preparing for potential threats, AI helps organizations stay ahead of cybercriminals, minimizing the time between an attack occurring and its mitigation.

Challenges and Limitations

Despite its significant benefits, the use of AI in threat detection and analysis does not come without its challenges. One of the main hurdles is the potential for false positives. While AI is designed to detect anomalies, there is still a risk that normal user behavior or network traffic might be flagged as suspicious. If these false positives are not managed effectively, they can overwhelm security teams and lead to alert fatigue.

Another challenge is ensuring that AI models remain unbiased and transparent. AI systems are only as effective as the data they are trained on, and if that data is incomplete or biased, it can lead to inaccurate threat detection or unjust decision-making. Ensuring that AI models are properly trained, tested, and updated regularly is critical to maintaining their effectiveness.

Additionally, AI-driven systems require significant computational resources, and implementing AI solutions can be costly for smaller organizations. The complexity of AI models may also require specialized knowledge to deploy, manage, and fine-tune.

Leveraging AI for threat detection and analysis is a game-changer in the fight against cybercrime. With its ability to detect emerging threats, automate responses, and enhance threat intelligence, AI is enabling organizations to proactively defend their networks against an increasingly sophisticated array of cyber-attacks. By harnessing the power of AI, organizations can stay one step ahead of cybercriminals, ensuring the security and resilience of their digital assets.

As AI technology continues to evolve, its role in cybersecurity will only expand. The integration of AI into threat detection and analysis systems is no longer just an option, it's a necessity for organizations that wish to stay protected in an era where cybercrime is pervasive and constantly evolving. By continuing to invest in AI-driven cybersecurity solutions, organizations can strengthen their defenses and mitigate risks before they materialize into costly breaches.

B. Machine Learning Models for Intrusion Detection

As cyber threats continue to evolve in both scale and sophistication, traditional methods of intrusion detection are often insufficient in identifying and mitigating modern, highly adaptive attacks. Intrusion Detection Systems (IDS) have become an essential component of a comprehensive cybersecurity strategy, tasked with monitoring network traffic and system behavior to detect any unusual or malicious activity. However, as the frequency and complexity of cyberattacks increase, relying on rule-based systems alone is no longer enough. Machine learning (ML) models have emerged as a powerful solution for enhancing intrusion detection systems, offering capabilities far beyond traditional methods.

Machine learning, a subset of artificial intelligence (AI), allows systems to learn from data and improve over time without explicit programming. By training on large datasets, machine learning models can identify patterns, anomalies, and trends that may indicate a security breach. In the context of intrusion detection, these models enable real-time analysis and response to threats, significantly improving the effectiveness and efficiency of security measures.

Types of Machine Learning Models for Intrusion Detection

Intrusion detection systems powered by machine learning use a variety of models to detect unauthorized access, data breaches, and other forms of malicious activity. Each type of model serves a different purpose, from anomaly detection to pattern recognition, ensuring a multi-faceted approach to identifying threats.

- **Supervised Learning Models**

Supervised learning is one of the most widely used techniques in intrusion detection. In supervised learning, the model is trained on a labeled dataset, where both normal and malicious behaviors are clearly marked. The system uses this dataset to learn the differences between legitimate and malicious activities. Once trained, the model can predict the likelihood of a given event being a potential security threat.

Common supervised learning algorithms used in intrusion detection include:

- **Decision Trees**: Decision trees are hierarchical models that classify network activities based on a series of decisions made at each node. Each decision involves evaluating specific features of the data, such as IP addresses, packet sizes, or connection types. Decision trees are easy to interpret and can quickly identify the most significant factors associated with an attack.
- **Support Vector Machines (SVM)**: Support vector machines are powerful classifiers that work by mapping

data points to a higher-dimensional space, where it becomes easier to distinguish between normal and malicious activity. SVMs are particularly effective in environments with complex and high-dimensional datasets, making them a popular choice for network traffic analysis.

- **Naive Bayes**: Based on Bayes' Theorem, Naive Bayes classifiers use the likelihood of an event occurring based on prior knowledge of similar events. This probabilistic approach can be used to identify malicious network activities, especially when the dataset includes various features such as packet details and timestamps.

- **Unsupervised Learning Models**

Unlike supervised learning, unsupervised learning does not require labeled data. Instead, these models learn to detect anomalies by analyzing the underlying structure of the data itself. This makes unsupervised models particularly useful when there is insufficient labeled data available or when the network environment is constantly changing, as in the case of zero-day attacks.

Common unsupervised learning techniques in intrusion detection include:

- **K-Means Clustering**: This algorithm groups similar data points together into clusters based on their characteristics. In the context of intrusion detection, K-means clustering can be used to identify network traffic patterns that deviate significantly from the norm, which may indicate an attack or an intrusion.

- **Isolation Forests**: Isolation forests are a model designed to identify anomalies by isolating data points that are different from the rest of the data. The algorithm works by partitioning the data into smaller subsets and measuring how easy it is to isolate individual points. Outliers that are harder to isolate are flagged as potential threats.

- **Reinforcement Learning Models**

Reinforcement learning (RL) is a type of machine learning where the system learns through interaction with its environment, making decisions and receiving feedback based on the outcomes of those decisions. In the case of intrusion detection, RL models can be used to continuously adapt to new attack patterns, improving the system's response to threats over time.

Reinforcement learning models are particularly beneficial in environments where the threat landscape is dynamic, as they allow intrusion detection systems to "learn" from new attack patterns in real-time. These models can be integrated into security systems that automatically respond to attacks by taking predefined actions, such as blocking malicious IP addresses or isolating infected devices.

Features Used in Machine Learning Models for Intrusion Detection

The effectiveness of machine learning models in intrusion detection depends heavily on the features selected for training. Features are the measurable characteristics or attributes of network traffic or system activity that are used to identify patterns of behavior. Some key features commonly used in machine learning-based intrusion detection systems include:

- **Packet Header Information**: Information such as source and destination IP addresses, ports, and protocol types can be used to detect suspicious activities such as port scanning or denial-of-service (DoS) attacks.

- **Traffic Volume**: Sudden spikes or drops in traffic volume can indicate anomalies, such as a DDoS attack or unauthorized data exfiltration. Machine learning models can use traffic patterns to flag these changes and prevent security breaches.

- **Session Duration and Frequency**: Abnormal session lengths or unusually frequent connections from the same source IP address can be indicative of malicious activities like brute force attacks or unauthorized access.

- **Payload Analysis**: The content of data packets can also be analyzed for malicious code or unusual patterns that may indicate malware or data tampering. ML models can detect abnormal payload content that deviates from established patterns.

Advantages of Machine Learning for Intrusion Detection

- Enhanced Accuracy and Precision

- Machine learning models, particularly when trained on large datasets, can provide high levels of accuracy and precision in detecting threats. These models continuously improve their ability to detect new and emerging threats based on patterns learned from past incidents. As a result, they are able to identify previously unknown attack vectors and rapidly adapt to new forms of intrusion.

- **Real-Time Detection and Mitigation**

- One of the significant advantages of machine learning-based intrusion detection systems is their ability to detect and respond to attacks in real-time. By continuously monitoring network traffic and system behavior, ML models can identify and mitigate threats as they occur, reducing the window of opportunity for attackers to exploit vulnerabilities.

- Reduced False Positives
- In traditional rule-based systems, false positives (incorrectly identifying legitimate activities as malicious) are a common problem. Machine learning models, however, are more adept at distinguishing between normal activities and actual threats. This helps reduce the number of false alarms and allows security teams to focus their attention on true incidents, increasing operational efficiency.
- Scalability and Adaptability
- Machine learning models can easily scale to accommodate larger datasets and complex environments. As the volume of network traffic increases, the models can handle the added data load without a significant drop in performance. Additionally, they can quickly adapt to new attack methods by learning from new data and emerging trends, making them highly adaptable to evolving threats.

Challenges and Considerations

While machine learning has proven to be an invaluable tool for intrusion detection, there are several challenges that must be addressed to fully leverage its capabilities:

- **Data Quality**: The quality of the training data is paramount in ensuring the effectiveness of machine learning models. Poor-quality or biased data can result in inaccurate predictions, leading to both false positives and false negatives.
- **Complexity of Deployment**: Implementing machine learning-based intrusion detection systems requires

significant expertise in data science, machine learning, and cybersecurity. Organizations must invest in skilled professionals and the necessary infrastructure to develop, train, and maintain these models.

- **Resource Intensive**: Machine learning models, particularly deep learning algorithms, can be computationally expensive and require substantial resources for training and deployment. Organizations must ensure that they have the necessary infrastructure to support these models.

Machine learning has fundamentally changed the landscape of intrusion detection, providing organizations with advanced tools to identify, analyze, and mitigate cyber threats in real time. By leveraging machine learning models for intrusion detection, organizations can gain deeper insights into network activity, improve the accuracy of threat detection, and reduce the impact of security breaches. While challenges remain, the continued evolution of machine learning and its integration into cybersecurity practices will continue to play a pivotal role in safeguarding digital assets and ensuring the integrity of critical systems. As cyber threats become more sophisticated, machine learning offers the best opportunity for staying ahead of attackers and enhancing the resilience of cybersecurity defenses.

C. Automating Digital Evidence Processing

The rapid evolution of cybercrime has increased the need for more efficient and scalable methods in digital forensics. Traditionally, forensic investigators meticulously analyzed digital evidence by hand, a process that could take weeks or even months. Today, advancements in artificial intelligence (AI) and machine learning (ML) are revolutionizing how digital evidence is processed, analyzed, and preserved. These technologies automate various aspects of the digital evidence life cycle, offering both efficiency and reliability, and helping investigators stay ahead of ever-evolving cyber threats.

Automated Tools for Data Collection and Preservation

Digital evidence must be collected and preserved in such a way that it can be used in court as part of legal proceedings. The process of digital evidence collection traditionally involved manually copying data from devices, preserving metadata, and ensuring the integrity of the evidence. However, modern automated tools are streamlining this process, making it faster and more reliable. AI-powered software can now scan digital devices, identify critical evidence, and create exact forensic copies of the data while maintaining the integrity of the original evidence. This automation reduces human error and ensures that evidence is preserved according to strict protocols, increasing the likelihood that it will be admissible in court.

Automated Evidence Analysis

Once evidence has been collected, the next step is analysis identifying relevant data, understanding the context of the evidence, and drawing conclusions that can aid in the investigation. Traditionally, forensic investigators sifted through terabytes of data manually, a daunting task that often led to overlooked evidence or delayed responses. AI-powered analysis tools are now capable of quickly processing and examining large volumes of data, identifying patterns, anomalies, and relationships that would be time-consuming for humans to uncover. Through techniques such as natural language processing (NLP), machine learning, and data mining, these tools can detect digital evidence such as hidden files, encrypted messages, or illicit communications.

Machine learning models can be trained to recognize specific types of cybercrime activities such as phishing, financial fraud, or malware distribution. This enables forensic teams to automate the detection of suspicious behavior in digital evidence with far greater speed and accuracy than traditional methods allowed. These tools provide investigators with prioritized findings, ensuring that the most important and relevant pieces of evidence are brought to the forefront for further analysis.

Integrating Automation in Incident Response

In addition to improving forensic analysis, automation is also playing a key role in incident response. By integrating automated digital evidence processing into incident response workflows, organizations can speed up their reaction time to cyber incidents. Automated systems can immediately begin collecting and analyzing evidence when an attack is detected, providing real-time insights into the nature of the threat and how it is progressing. This allows security teams to mitigate damage before the attacker can cause further harm.

In cases of large-scale cyberattacks such as Distributed Denial of Service (DDoS) or ransomware, automated tools can help identify the source of the attack, its entry points, and its spread throughout a network. Furthermore, AI-driven systems can be configured to automatically isolate infected systems and take other defensive actions, reducing the need for manual intervention and allowing forensic analysts to focus on higher-level decision-making.

The Role of Automation in Legal and Compliance Frameworks

Automated digital evidence processing doesn't just improve operational efficiency it also helps organizations maintain compliance with legal and regulatory frameworks. In jurisdictions where data protection laws like the General Data Protection Regulation (GDPR) exist, automation ensures that evidence is handled in a way that respects the privacy of individuals and adheres to privacy regulations. Automated systems are designed to track how digital evidence is handled and ensure that every step of the process is documented for accountability.

Additionally, AI-powered tools can ensure that investigators follow proper chain-of-custody procedures. The automated system can create a detailed log of when, where, and how evidence was collected, analyzed, and stored, minimizing the risk of tampering or loss. This transparency is critical for ensuring that digital evidence is handled in a way that meets legal standards.

The Challenges and Ethical Considerations

While automation in digital evidence processing offers numerous advantages, it also introduces new challenges. One of the most pressing concerns is the potential for bias in AI systems. Machine learning models are only as good as the data they are trained on, and if these models are trained on biased data, they may produce flawed or incomplete results. For example, if a model is trained predominantly on data from one geographic region or type of cybercrime, it may struggle to identify threats from other regions or emerging attack techniques.

Another ethical consideration is the transparency of AI algorithms. Investigators and organizations must ensure that automated systems are understandable and explainable. This is important not only for verifying the accuracy of results but also for maintaining public trust in digital forensics processes. If the decision-making process behind an AI algorithm is opaque, it may be difficult to defend the results in a court of law.

Furthermore, the automation of digital evidence processing raises questions about data security and privacy. While automation tools help ensure the integrity of evidence, they also increase the potential for large-scale data breaches if they are not properly secured. As AI and automation become more integral to cybersecurity, there is an increasing need for strong security practices to protect the integrity of evidence and the confidentiality of sensitive data.

The Future of Automated Digital Evidence Processing

Looking ahead, automated digital evidence processing is expected to continue evolving and becoming more sophisticated. Advancements in AI, machine learning, and natural language processing will enable even more precise and rapid analysis of digital evidence. These technologies are poised to help forensic investigators and cybersecurity professionals stay ahead of cybercriminals by identifying threats before they materialize, improving the accuracy and speed of investigations, and enhancing the security of digital infrastructures.

Moreover, as automation in cyber forensics continues to mature, the integration of AI and machine learning with blockchain and other emerging technologies will further transform how digital evidence is handled. Blockchain, for instance, offers a secure and immutable way of recording data transactions, which could provide an added layer of security in tracking the chain of custody for digital evidence.

Ultimately, automation will empower cybersecurity professionals and forensic analysts with the tools they need to conduct more thorough, efficient, and timely investigations.

By streamlining digital evidence processing, AI and machine learning are set to redefine the field of cyber forensics, making it more agile, effective, and capable of responding to increasingly complex cybercrime. As organizations embrace these innovations, they will be better equipped to prevent, detect, and respond to cyber threats, ensuring a safer and more secure digital future.

CHAPTER FOUR

Forensic Investigation Methodologies and Tools

Cyber forensics is a complex and dynamic field, requiring a deep understanding of investigation methodologies and an arsenal of specialized tools to uncover evidence of cybercrime. Forensic investigations in the digital realm go far beyond simply retrieving data from a hard drive or analyzing network logs. They require a precise, methodical approach to collect, preserve, and analyze evidence that is often fragmented across multiple systems, devices, and platforms. As technology advances, forensic investigators are faced with new challenges and opportunities to refine their methodologies and adopt new tools that aid in their efforts.

The ultimate goal of forensic investigation is to present findings that are not only accurate but legally defensible. In order to achieve this, investigators must adhere to strict procedures that ensure the integrity of the evidence throughout the investigation process. The forensic investigation methodology follows a structured framework, incorporating evidence gathering, data analysis, and reporting, all while ensuring that the digital evidence remains unaltered and admissible in a court of law.

Digital Evidence Collection and Preservation

One of the most critical stages in any forensic investigation is the collection and preservation of digital evidence. Investigators must take great care to ensure that evidence is gathered in a manner that maintains its integrity and chain of custody. This process involves carefully acquiring data from various sources, such as hard drives, cloud storage, mobile devices, network traffic, and even Internet of Things (IoT) devices, without altering or damaging the original data.

The first step in the process is identifying the sources of potential evidence, which may include both primary and secondary sources. Primary sources are those that are most directly related to the incident, such as a compromised server or a hacked endpoint. Secondary sources might include auxiliary devices like backup drives, logs, or communications between perpetrators. Once these sources are identified, investigators must use forensic imaging techniques to create exact copies (or "images") of the original data, ensuring that the original data remains untouched during the analysis.

Forensic investigators must also adhere to legal and regulatory requirements when collecting and preserving evidence. The chain of custody documentation is essential in maintaining a clear record of who has handled the evidence and at what point in time. This ensures that the evidence cannot be disputed in court, as it guarantees that the data has remained intact and unaltered throughout the investigation.

Data Analysis Techniques

Once the evidence has been collected, forensic investigators employ a range of analytical techniques to uncover relevant information that can shed light on the events surrounding the cybercrime. These techniques can be broadly categorized into three types: static analysis, dynamic analysis, and network analysis.

- **Static Analysis**: Static analysis involves examining data that is not actively running or in use. This includes analyzing file systems, data structures, and system images to identify malicious files, unauthorized access, or traces of cybercriminal activity. Static analysis is often used to examine malware; decrypt encrypted files and recover deleted data from storage devices.

- **Dynamic Analysis**: Dynamic analysis focuses on analyzing live systems or real-time data. This includes monitoring the behavior of applications, processes, and network traffic while they are running. Dynamic analysis is particularly useful for studying the behavior of malware, understanding how cybercriminals interact with a system, and identifying vulnerabilities in real time. Forensic investigators often use sandbox environments to safely observe malware in action without risking damage to the host system.

- **Network Analysis**: Network analysis is critical in cyber forensics, as many attacks involve manipulation of network traffic. Investigators use packet capture tools, such as Wireshark, to analyze network traffic and identify malicious communications, data exfiltration attempts, and unauthorized access points. Network analysis can reveal how an attacker gained access to a network, what systems were targeted, and the extent of the compromise.

Forensic Investigation Tools

To conduct effective forensic investigations, digital forensics experts rely on a variety of specialized tools. These tools range from general-purpose software suites to highly specialized applications designed to handle specific types of data or investigations. Some of the most widely used forensic investigation tools include:

- **EnCase**: EnCase is one of the most popular forensic tools used in law enforcement and corporate cybersecurity investigations. It allows investigators to create forensic images of digital devices, recover deleted files, and analyze file systems. EnCase supports a wide range of file systems and provides powerful reporting capabilities.
- **FTK (Forensic Toolkit)**: FTK is another widely used digital forensics software suite. It offers capabilities for data imaging, file analysis, and email investigations. FTK's data carving features allow investigators to recover deleted files, even if they have been partially overwritten, while its built-in search and analysis tools make it easy to identify patterns in large datasets.
- **Autopsy**: Autopsy is an open-source forensic analysis tool that supports file system analysis, timeline creation, and keyword searching. It is commonly used for examining digital evidence in criminal investigations and is known for its user-friendly interface. Autopsy supports a wide range of formats and devices, including hard drives, mobile devices, and cloud storage.
- **Wireshark**: Wireshark is a powerful network analysis tool used to capture and examine network traffic. It is often employed in forensic investigations to analyze communication patterns, detect anomalies, and identify signs of data exfiltration. Wireshark provides investigators with detailed packet-level data, which can be crucial for uncovering how an attack unfolded.
- **X1 Social Discovery**: In cases involving social media or online communications, X1 Social Discovery is an essential tool. It allows investigators to collect and analyze data from a wide range of social media platforms, including Facebook, Twitter, and Instagram. The tool can also be used to collect

evidence from email accounts and cloud services, providing a comprehensive view of online activity.

- **Volatility**: Volatility is an open-source memory forensics tool used to analyze volatile data from live systems, such as RAM. Memory forensics is crucial for analyzing malware that operates in memory and identifying artifacts that may not be visible on the file system. Volatility enables investigators to extract valuable information from memory dumps, including running processes, network connections, and encryption keys.

- **Cellebrite**: In mobile device forensics, Cellebrite is a leading tool used to extract data from smartphones, tablets, and other mobile devices. It supports a wide variety of operating systems and allows investigators to retrieve deleted messages, call logs, photos, and other data that may be crucial to the investigation.

- **OSForensics**: Forensics is a comprehensive digital forensics tool that offers capabilities for file analysis, data carving, password recovery, and email investigations. It allows investigators to search for evidence across multiple devices and platforms, and it features advanced tools for hashing and encryption analysis.

The Role of Automation in Forensic Investigations

The growing complexity of cybercrime and the vast amounts of data generated by digital systems have made forensic investigations increasingly challenging. Automation plays a crucial role in handling large-scale investigations by streamlining routine tasks and increasing efficiency.

For example, automated data collection tools can help investigators acquire forensic images and evidence quickly, without the need for manual intervention. Automation can also aid in the initial analysis of data, flagging potential leads for further investigation. Additionally, automation tools can assist in reporting and documentation, ensuring that every step of the investigation is accurately recorded and ready for legal proceedings.

The integration of machine learning and AI into forensic tools has also enhanced the ability to automatically detect patterns, anomalies, and malicious activity. As AI algorithms improve, they will play an increasingly significant role in automating data analysis, allowing forensic investigators to focus on higher-level investigative tasks.

Forensic investigation methodologies and tools are essential components of modern cyber forensics. The tools and techniques used by investigators enable them to uncover hidden evidence, analyze attack patterns, and provide actionable insights that help organizations mitigate risks and protect against cybercrime. As cyber threats continue to evolve, forensic investigators must stay up to date with the latest tools and methodologies to ensure they are prepared to tackle the challenges of the digital age. By utilizing the right tools and following established investigative protocols, forensic professionals can maintain the integrity of their findings and provide accurate, actionable results in the pursuit of justice.

- **Cyber Forensic Process: Identification, Collection, Analysis, and Reporting**

In the world of cybersecurity, effective forensic investigations are essential for identifying, understanding, and mitigating cybercrimes. The process of digital forensics involves a series of meticulous steps to ensure that evidence is handled, preserved, and analyzed in a manner that is both legally and scientifically sound. These steps form a structured approach to digital crime investigation, ensuring that the integrity of the data remains intact throughout the process. In this section, we will delve into the core stages of the cyber forensic process identification, collection, analysis, and reporting highlighting the importance of each stage in building a robust case against cybercriminals.

1. Identification: Uncovering Potential Evidence

The first step in the cyber forensic process is identification. This phase is critical because it lays the foundation for the entire investigation. During identification, forensic experts focus on determining the scope of the incident, locating the systems and devices involved, and pinpointing the data that may contain evidence of the attack. In this phase, investigators must identify key assets such as servers, endpoints, network traffic logs, and cloud-based systems that could hold valuable forensic evidence.

This step also involves determining the type of cybercrime that has occurred whether it's a data breach, malware attack, insider threat, or some other form of cybercrime. Identifying the affected systems helps forensic experts understand the nature of the crime, the potential suspects, and the impact on the organization's digital infrastructure. Without accurate identification, subsequent steps in the investigation may lead to incomplete or irrelevant evidence, which could hinder the investigation and prosecution of the attackers.

One of the primary challenges in this phase is managing the scale of digital systems and data involved. Modern networks often consist of complex environments, including cloud systems, IoT devices, and mobile platforms, all of which may have been compromised. Forensic investigators must thoroughly understand the interconnectedness of these systems and pinpoint the exact locations of digital evidence.

2. Collection: Safeguarding and Preserving Evidence

Once potential evidence has been identified, the next critical step is the collection of that evidence. This phase is pivotal to the success of any cyber forensic investigation because the integrity of digital evidence can be easily compromised if not handled properly. Forensic investigators must ensure that the collection process is thorough, systematic, and conducted with legal and procedural diligence.

The collection of digital evidence requires that investigators preserve the original state of the data, ensuring that it remains unaltered and admissible in a court of law. To do this, investigators follow a strict chain of custody protocol, documenting each step of the process to ensure that every action is traceable. They utilize specialized tools and techniques to create forensic images or copies of devices, ensuring that the original data is preserved, and no alterations are made during the investigation.

Forensic investigators collect a wide range of digital evidence, including hard drives, memory chips, system logs, network traffic data, and email records. Additionally, investigators may collect metadata, such as timestamps and access logs, which can provide valuable insights into the sequence of events leading up to or following the cybercrime. Physical evidence, such as devices or hardware used in the attack, may also be collected if necessary.

It is essential that investigators approach the collection phase with precision. Any improper handling or unauthorized access to evidence can lead to accusations of tampering, which could damage the credibility of the investigation. Furthermore, any errors in the chain of custody can undermine the integrity of the evidence, potentially rendering it inadmissible in legal proceedings.

3. Analysis: Extracting Meaning from the Data

Once the evidence has been identified and collected, the next step is analysis. This is the stage where forensic experts examine the digital evidence to uncover the full scope of the incident, trace the attacker's actions, and identify any patterns that could help in solving the case. The analysis phase is often the most time-consuming and complex part of the forensic process, as it involves sifting through vast amounts of data to identify useful information.

Forensic investigators use specialized software tools to examine and analyze digital evidence. These tools allow them to recover deleted files, examine encrypted data, and search for traces of malicious activities. Investigators analyze network traffic, system logs, application data, and file systems to determine how the attack occurred, what vulnerabilities were exploited, and which systems were impacted.

One of the key elements of the analysis phase is correlation. Investigators must correlate data from different sources to build a coherent timeline of events. For example, analyzing system logs from servers and comparing them to network traffic data can reveal the exact time and manner in which the attack was initiated and how it propagated across the network. The ability to piece together information from various sources enables investigators to reconstruct the attack with high precision.

In cases of malware or ransomware attacks, the analysis phase can involve reverse-engineering the malicious code to understand its functionality, origin, and potential impact.

This detailed analysis can provide crucial information about the attacker's tactics, techniques, and procedures (TTPs), which can then be used to prevent similar attacks in the future.

4. Reporting: Documenting Findings and Recommendations

The final step in the cyber forensic process is reporting. Once the analysis has been completed, forensic investigators must document their findings in a clear, concise, and comprehensible manner. A well-written forensic report serves as a formal record of the investigation and provides crucial information for stakeholders, law enforcement, and legal teams.

Forensic reports should include a detailed timeline of events, an overview of the evidence collected, and a thorough analysis of the findings. The report should also document any actions taken during the investigation, including steps to preserve evidence, forensic imaging, and tools used for analysis. In cases involving criminal activity, the report must be carefully structured to ensure that the evidence is admissible in court.

In addition to documenting the investigation's findings, the report should offer recommendations for improving security measures and mitigating future risks. For example, the report may suggest changes to network configurations, better user access controls, or updated security protocols to prevent similar cyberattacks from occurring in the future.

Forensic investigators must ensure that their reports are objective, factual, and free from bias. The clarity and precision of the report are essential, especially when the findings are used in legal proceedings. A well-prepared report can help establish the cause of the cybercrime, link the attacker to the crime, and strengthen the case for prosecution.

The cyber forensic process comprising identification, collection, analysis, and reporting is a critical framework for investigating and solving cybercrimes. Each phase is built upon the previous one, ensuring that digital evidence is handled with care, integrity, and precision. By following this structured approach, forensic investigators can uncover the truth behind cyberattacks, provide valuable insights into the methods used by cybercriminals, and help organizations strengthen their defenses against future attacks. As cybercrime becomes more complex, the importance of robust forensic processes in digital investigations will only continue to grow.

- **Essential Tools for Digital Forensics (e.g., Autopsy, FTK, EnCase)**

Digital forensics is a discipline that hinges not only on methodologies and investigative rigor but also on the strength and sophistication of the tools employed. As cybercrime grows in complexity, the need for reliable, scalable, and court-admissible forensic tools becomes increasingly crucial. These tools serve as the backbone of forensic investigations enabling experts to uncover hidden data, trace malicious activity, and build defensible evidence chains in both corporate and criminal settings. Among the vast array of available solutions, Autopsy, FTK (Forensic Toolkit), and EnCase have emerged as industry leaders, each offering distinct advantages suited to varying investigative needs.

Autopsy: Open-Source Forensic Powerhouse

Autopsy is a highly regarded open-source digital forensics platform developed by Basis Technology. Built on top of The Sleuth Kit, it provides a user-friendly graphical interface for conducting comprehensive forensic examinations. One of Autopsy's standout features is its modularity. It supports a variety of plugins for tasks such as keyword searches, timeline analysis, file carving, email parsing, and hash filtering.

Autopsy excels in disk image analysis, enabling investigators to mount and inspect file systems from compromised or suspicious machines. The platform also facilitates live keyword searching, metadata extraction, and email analysis, making it ideal for rapid-response investigations. Its integration with third-party modules allows for custom workflows and automation, while its affordability and community support make it accessible to forensic teams of all sizes, from law enforcement agencies to private investigators.

Despite being open-source, Autopsy is robust enough for courtroom use when properly applied. Its transparent logging and documentation features ensure that every step taken in the investigation can be audited and justified, maintaining evidentiary integrity throughout the investigative process.

FTK (Forensic Toolkit): Enterprise-Grade Speed and Indexing

Developed by Access Data, FTK is a commercial digital forensics suite known for its speed, processing efficiency, and powerful indexing capabilities. What distinguishes FTK is its focus on rapid, large-scale forensic analysis making it particularly effective for investigations involving voluminous datasets, such as corporate email archives, internal network breaches, or massive disk acquisitions.

FTK's engine is designed to pre-index all data, which drastically reduces search times and enhances data sorting during analysis. It supports advanced features such as file carving, registry analysis, timeline construction, and password cracking, while also providing built-in visualization tools that allow investigators to map relationships and identify behavioral patterns across devices and users.

For enterprise environments, FTK's case management capabilities shine. It allows multiple analysts to collaborate on a case simultaneously, ensuring synchronized workflows and shared insights. Additionally, its integration with Access Data's Lab and AD Enterprise tools enables remote data acquisition and live analysis, critical for corporate forensic teams managing distributed systems.

Its forensic imaging capabilities are forensically sound and support a wide array of formats, ensuring compatibility with different systems and evidence types. FTK's audit trails, encryption support, and reporting features are compliant with legal standards, allowing evidence to be presented in court with full confidence.

EnCase: The Gold Standard in Forensic Investigations

Guidance Software's EnCase has long been regarded as the gold standard in digital forensics, particularly within legal, law enforcement, and government sectors. Known for its comprehensive features and reliability, EnCase provides investigators with complete control over the digital evidence lifecycle from acquisition and analysis to reporting and courtroom presentation.

EnCase supports disk-level imaging and analysis of a broad range of digital devices, including computers, servers, and mobile phones. One of its key strengths lies in its deep-dive capability: investigators can recover deleted files, examine hidden partitions, inspect volatile memory, and perform encrypted file analysis with high precision. Its scripting engine and custom modules also allow advanced users to create tailored investigations, fine-tuned to specific cases or threats.

The EnCase Evidence File (E01) format is widely accepted in courts and law enforcement circles due to its built-in verification, compression, and documentation features. This makes EnCase not only a trusted tool for forensic examiners but also a bridge between technical investigators and legal professionals.

Another major advantage of EnCase is its support for both proactive and reactive investigations. Whether conducting a real-time response to a cyber incident or performing retrospective digital forensics, EnCase provides a structured and forensically sound environment for deep, defensible analysis.

The Role of Tool Selection in Forensic Success

Choosing the right forensic tool depends on the scope of the investigation, the complexity of the data involved, and the environment in which the investigation is conducted. While Autopsy may be ideal for budget-conscious or initial investigations, FTK and EnCase are often favored for enterprise-grade or high-stakes legal scenarios. The effectiveness of any tool, however, is largely determined by the skill and methodology of the forensic analyst using it.

Forensic tools must also align with legal and ethical standards. Each step taken with these tools must be auditable, reproducible, and defensible in a court of law. This underscores the importance of using tools that are not only powerful but also built with compliance, chain-of-custody preservation, and reporting in mind.

Interoperability and Integration

In modern forensic workflows, no single tool can cover every need. For this reason, interoperability between tools is a growing requirement. Analysts often use multiple tools in tandem Autopsy for initial triage, FTK for high-speed indexing and searches, and EnCase for in-depth disk and memory analysis. Integration with other platforms, such as SIEM systems, threat intelligence databases, or case management tools, further enhances the value of these forensic suites.

With cybercrime investigations becoming more intricate and multifaceted, the ability to extract, analyze, correlate, and preserve digital evidence efficiently is more important than ever. Autopsy, FTK, and EnCase each represent critical assets in the digital investigator's toolkit serving distinct purposes but united by a shared goal: uncovering the truth hidden within digital systems and ensuring justice in the digital age.

- **AI-Powered Forensic Analysis and Predictive Analytics**

In the digital age, the increasing sophistication and volume of cybercrimes require new methods for detecting, analyzing, and preventing attacks. Traditional forensic analysis, while effective, can be time-consuming and limited by the vast amounts of data that need to be processed. Enter artificial intelligence (AI) a transformative force in the field of cyber forensics. AI-powered forensic analysis and predictive analytics are revolutionizing the way investigators approach digital crime by enabling faster, more accurate, and more comprehensive examinations of complex data sets. These technologies provide cybersecurity professionals with tools to not only respond to incidents but to predict and prevent potential attacks.

AI-Powered Forensic Analysis Accelerating Investigations

AI has the potential to dramatically streamline the forensic investigation process. Traditional forensic methods often involve manually sifting through enormous amounts of data, such as logs, communications, file systems, and network traffic, to identify suspicious activity or potential threats. This process can be slow and error-prone, particularly when investigators are dealing with large-scale data from multiple sources.

AI-powered forensic analysis, however, leverages machine learning (ML) algorithms, natural language processing (NLP), and pattern recognition to automatically analyze digital evidence at a scale and speed that human investigators cannot match. These AI tools can process massive volumes of data from various sources files, emails, logs, network traffic, and more in a fraction of the time it would take traditional methods. By applying sophisticated algorithms, AI systems can identify patterns and anomalies that might otherwise go unnoticed.

For example, AI can be used to identify unusual access patterns or data exfiltration activities across a network, detect changes in file systems that may indicate malicious activity, or flag anomalous behavior within cloud environments. By doing so, AI allows investigators to focus on the most critical pieces of evidence, enhancing both the efficiency and accuracy of the investigation.

Furthermore, AI tools can be trained to recognize and categorize different types of cybercrimes, such as phishing, malware infections, and data breaches, making it easier for investigators to determine the nature of an attack and respond accordingly. As AI systems learn from previous cases and vast datasets, they become more adept at spotting new types of attacks, continually improving the forensic investigation process.

Predictive Analytics: Foreseeing Future Attacks

While forensic analysis helps to understand past cybercrimes, predictive analytics uses AI to forecast future threats and vulnerabilities, providing cybersecurity teams with a proactive advantage. Predictive analytics involves analyzing historical data and identifying patterns to predict where, when, and how cyberattacks are likely to occur in the future. This forward-looking approach allows organizations to strengthen their defenses before attacks take place, rather than only reacting after the fact.

AI-powered predictive analytics tools can process vast amounts of structured and unstructured data, including system logs, network traffic, threat intelligence feeds, and even external data sources, such as dark web activity or hacker forums. By analyzing this data, predictive models can identify emerging trends and vulnerabilities that may lead to future cybercrimes. These tools can recognize recurring attack vectors, the evolution of malware, or common tactics used by cybercriminals, providing critical insights into potential future threats.

For example, predictive models can forecast when a specific vulnerability will be exploited based on historical data, threat actor behavior, and global trends. This allows security teams to implement targeted patches and preventive measures before cybercriminals can take advantage of the weakness. Similarly, predictive analytics can help organizations identify which systems are most likely to be targeted in a cyberattack, allowing for more focused defenses and resource allocation.

Predictive analytics also plays a significant role in threat intelligence. By leveraging AI to analyze large sets of threat intelligence data, organizations can identify early signs of coordinated attacks, such as those carried out by advanced persistent threats (APTs). This early warning system enables cybersecurity teams to act quickly, thwarting the attack before significant damage occurs.

AI and Predictive Analytics in Malware and Ransomware Detection

One of the most significant benefits of AI-powered forensic analysis and predictive analytics is their ability to detect malware and ransomware attacks at early stages. Traditional antivirus software relies heavily on signature-based detection, which requires identifying known malware signatures. However, this approach is often ineffective against new or unknown threats, such as zero-day vulnerabilities or polymorphic malware that changes its code to evade detection.

AI-driven solutions, on the other hand, can detect anomalous behaviors and patterns within systems, such as unusual file modifications, encryption activities, or unexpected network traffic, which may indicate a malware or ransomware attack. These AI systems do not require prior knowledge of the malware itself. Instead, they continuously learn from the data and adapt to detect new, previously unknown attack methods. This behavior-based detection capability is crucial for identifying and mitigating attacks in real time.

Moreover, predictive analytics can play an essential role in ransomware prevention. By analyzing patterns of ransomware activity, AI models can predict when an organization is at risk of an attack. For instance, predictive models can assess network traffic, identify weak points in the network, and flag areas that are particularly vulnerable to ransomware infiltration. Armed with this knowledge, organizations can take preemptive steps to block the attack, such as by isolating vulnerable systems or applying stronger security measures.

Enhancing Incident Response with AI and Predictive Insights

AI and predictive analytics also enhance incident response capabilities. In the event of a cyberattack, these technologies can help security teams make informed decisions faster, reducing response times and minimizing the damage caused by the attack. AI can assist in automatically classifying the severity of an attack, identifying which systems have been compromised, and determining the root cause of the incident.

Furthermore, predictive analytics can guide incident response efforts by forecasting the potential consequences of an attack based on past incidents and data. For example, predictive models may predict the spread of an attack across the network, helping response teams prioritize containment efforts and direct resources to critical areas. This predictive insight can improve the accuracy and effectiveness of incident response, helping organizations recover more quickly and reduce the overall impact of the attack.

Challenges and Ethical Considerations in AI-Powered Forensic Analysis

While AI and predictive analytics offer transformative potential for cyber forensics, there are several challenges and ethical considerations that must be addressed. One of the primary concerns is the need for high-quality, unbiased data. AI systems are only as effective as the data they are trained on, and poor-quality or biased data can lead to inaccurate predictions or missed detections. Ensuring that AI systems are trained on comprehensive and diverse datasets is essential for achieving reliable results.

Another challenge is the transparency and explainability of AI models. Many AI systems, particularly deep learning models, operate as "black boxes," meaning that their decision-making processes are not easily understood by human investigators. This lack of transparency can be problematic, especially in legal contexts where the chain of custody and admissibility of evidence is critical. It is essential for cybersecurity professionals to ensure that AI-driven forensic tools are transparent and that their decisions can be explained and justified in a legal setting.

Finally, there are privacy and data protection concerns when using AI in cyber forensics. AI systems often require access to large datasets, which may include sensitive personal or corporate information. Ensuring that AI tools comply with privacy regulations, such as GDPR or CCPA, is crucial to maintaining the ethical integrity of the investigation and protecting the rights of individuals.

AI-powered forensic analysis and predictive analytics are revolutionizing the field of cyber forensics by enabling faster, more accurate, and proactive threat detection and analysis. These technologies offer significant advantages over traditional forensic methods, from identifying patterns in large datasets to predicting future attacks and preventing cybercrimes before they occur. By leveraging AI in the forensic investigation process, organizations can enhance their cyber resilience, reduce response times, and improve their overall security posture. However, it is essential to address challenges such as data quality, model transparency, and ethical considerations to ensure the responsible and effective use of

AI in cyber forensics. As AI continues to evolve, its role in the future of digital security will only become more indispensable, shaping the way cybersecurity professionals tackle cybercrime and protect digital infrastructures worldwide.

CHAPTER FIVE
Network Security and Threat Intelligence

In the constantly shifting terrain of cyberspace, network security serves as the frontline defense against a vast array of digital threats. With enterprises becoming increasingly interconnected and reliant on digital infrastructure, the importance of securing networks cannot be overstated. A single vulnerability in a network's configuration can provide cybercriminals with a gateway to sensitive data, critical systems, and even national infrastructure. As such, network security is no longer just a technical requirement, it is a foundational element of any cybersecurity strategy.

Effective network security goes beyond firewalls and antivirus software; it encompasses a holistic architecture that includes intrusion detection systems (IDS), intrusion prevention systems (IPS), endpoint protection, encryption, secure access controls, and continuous monitoring. Organizations must adopt layered security approaches often referred to as "defense in depth" to build resilience against sophisticated and persistent threats. This strategy ensures that if one layer is breached, others remain to protect vital assets.

Network threats have evolved in both complexity and scale. From traditional malware and phishing attacks to more advanced persistent threats (APTs) and zero-day exploits, attackers are constantly devising new ways to infiltrate and exploit networks. Complicating matters further, many attacks now leverage encrypted traffic to bypass conventional detection systems, making the role of intelligent monitoring tools and behavioral analytics more critical than ever.

This is where threat intelligence comes into play. Threat intelligence refers to the collection and analysis of data about potential or active threats that could affect an organization's digital environment. It offers actionable insights into the tactics, techniques, and procedures (TTPs) used by threat actors, allowing organizations to prepare proactively and respond effectively. Rather than being reactive, security teams empowered with high-quality threat intelligence can anticipate attacks and implement countermeasures before damage is done.

There are three primary types of threat intelligence: strategic, tactical, and operational. Strategic intelligence provides a high-level overview of threat landscapes, often used by executives and decision-makers to guide cybersecurity policy and investments. Tactical intelligence focuses on the methods used by attackers, such as phishing schemes or malware deployment strategies. Operational intelligence delivers real-time information that supports immediate responses, such as identifying a newly launched botnet or a zero-day exploit in circulation.

Modern network defense also involves sharing threat intelligence across organizations and industries. Collaborative threat intelligence platforms allow cybersecurity professionals to pool knowledge and accelerate detection and response. Initiatives such as Information Sharing and Analysis Centers (ISACs) and global threat-sharing alliances strengthen collective cyber resilience by ensuring that no organization faces threats in isolation.

Artificial intelligence and machine learning are playing transformative roles in both network security and threat intelligence. AI-driven security systems are capable of identifying anomalies, recognizing patterns indicative of malicious behavior, and automating responses to incidents. These systems continuously learn from new data, improving their detection capabilities over time and reducing the dwell time of attackers within networks. Machine learning models can sift through massive volumes of network traffic, detect subtle indicators of compromise (IoCs), and prioritize threats based on risk level and potential impact.

The integration of threat intelligence into security information and event management (SIEM) platforms further enhances the ability of organizations to detect and respond to network threats. SIEM tools aggregate logs and alerts from across the infrastructure and correlate them with threat intelligence feeds to provide context and visibility. This unified view helps security analysts understand not only that an incident has occurred, but also the likely motivations, techniques, and objectives behind it.

Securing a network also involves building robust incident response protocols and disaster recovery plans. In the event of a breach, having well-documented and rehearsed response strategies can significantly limit damage, contain the threat, and facilitate rapid recovery. This includes identifying the affected systems, isolating compromised segments of the network, communicating with stakeholders, and preserving digital evidence for forensic analysis.

Moreover, as remote work and cloud computing become the norm, securing network perimeters is no longer sufficient. Organizations must adopt a zero-trust architecture, where no user or device is inherently trusted, even if it operates inside the network perimeter. Zero trust enforces strict identity verification, least privilege access, and continuous monitoring, drastically reducing the attack surface.

Ultimately, network security and threat intelligence are not isolated functions, they are interdependent pillars of a broader cybersecurity strategy. Threat intelligence informs security policies and detection mechanisms, while robust network defenses provide the necessary infrastructure to implement and enforce those policies. Together, they enable organizations to move from a reactive posture to a proactive, intelligence-led approach to cybersecurity.

As the volume and velocity of cyber threats continue to grow, too must the capabilities of network security systems and threat intelligence operations. Investing in these areas is not merely a technological decision but a strategic imperative for any entity that values the security, privacy, and continuity of its digital operations. By embracing a data-driven, intelligence-informed model of defense, cybersecurity professionals can safeguard networks against even the most elusive adversaries today and in the evolving threat landscapes of tomorrow.

A. AI-Driven Threat Intelligence Frameworks

In the ever-evolving domain of cybersecurity, threat intelligence has emerged as a critical pillar for identifying, understanding, and mitigating potential risks. The rapid advancement of cyber threats ranging from zero-day vulnerabilities and ransomware campaigns to nation-state attacks necessitates a more dynamic, automated, and intelligent approach to gathering and acting upon threat data. AI-driven threat intelligence frameworks are at the forefront of this transformation, offering organizations the ability to process vast amounts of threat-related data with speed, precision, and strategic foresight.

Unlike traditional threat intelligence systems, which often rely on static indicators and manual analyses, AI-infused frameworks continuously learn from new data, adapt to changing threat environments, and generate actionable insights in real time. These systems not only enhance an organization's situational awareness but also empower security teams to anticipate attacker behavior, prioritize vulnerabilities, and implement countermeasures with unprecedented agility.

The Architecture of an AI-Driven Threat Intelligence Framework

An AI-driven threat intelligence framework is built upon several integrated layers that work cohesively to gather, process, analyze, and disseminate security insights. At its core lies the data ingestion engine, which pulls structured and unstructured data from a variety of sources: security information and event management (SIEM) systems, endpoint detection and response (EDR) tools, intrusion detection systems (IDS), threat feeds, open-source intelligence (OSINT), and dark web monitoring platforms.

Once collected, this raw data is processed using natural language processing (NLP), machine learning (ML), and deep learning models. NLP algorithms are particularly effective in parsing threat reports, hacker forums, and dark web communications to extract relevant entities such as IP addresses, malware hashes, tactics, techniques, and procedures (TTPs). Meanwhile, ML models analyze behavioral patterns, cluster similar threats, and identify anomalies that may signal emerging threats or coordinated attacks.

The output of this analysis is then translated into actionable threat intelligence through contextualization and prioritization. This step is vital for reducing alert fatigue and ensuring that security teams focus their attention on the most pressing and relevant threats. Through risk scoring and impact analysis, AI frameworks help decision-makers determine which vulnerabilities pose the greatest risk to their digital infrastructure, enabling targeted response and remediation efforts.

Enhancing Threat Detection and Attribution

One of the most powerful applications of AI in threat intelligence lies in its ability to detect sophisticated, stealthy threats that evade traditional detection methods. AI-driven frameworks can uncover subtle behavioral indicators such as lateral movement within a network, command-and-control communications, or abnormal user activity that may go unnoticed by signature-based tools.

Moreover, AI enhances the process of threat attribution by correlating indicators of compromise (IOCs) with known threat actor profiles and campaign patterns. By analyzing vast repositories of historical threat data, AI can link current incidents to specific threat groups, providing valuable context about their motivations, methods, and previous targets. This insight not only informs tactical response but also supports strategic planning and geopolitical risk assessments.

For example, if a machine learning model identifies that a newly discovered malware variant shares code similarities with a known advanced persistent threat (APT) campaign, security teams can proactively implement controls designed to mitigate tactics used by that specific group. This level of predictive capability is critical in staying ahead of sophisticated attackers who continuously evolve their techniques to bypass conventional defenses.

Automating Intelligence Sharing and Collaboration

Cyber threats often transcend organizational and geographic boundaries, making collaboration and information sharing essential. AI-driven threat intelligence frameworks facilitate real-time intelligence sharing between organizations, sectors, and national security entities without compromising confidentiality or operational integrity. Through standardized formats such as STIX (Structured Threat Information eXpression) and TAXII (Trusted Automated Exchange of Intelligence Information), AI can automatically package and transmit intelligence findings to trusted partners and consortiums.

This automation ensures that when one entity detects a new threat, others in the network are instantly alerted, creating a collective defense ecosystem. AI also helps reduce redundant data and false positives, ensuring that shared intelligence remains accurate and actionable. In regulated industries such as finance, healthcare, and critical infrastructure this real-time intelligence exchange is invaluable in fortifying supply chains, reducing attack surfaces, and meeting compliance requirements.

Real-Time Response and Adaptive Defense

The integration of AI threat intelligence with security orchestration, automation, and response (SOAR) platforms takes cyber defense to a new level of responsiveness. AI-enabled frameworks can trigger automated workflows when specific threat indicators are identified, such as isolating affected endpoints, blocking malicious IP addresses, or deploying patches to vulnerable systems. This rapid, automated response reduces dwell time and limits the scope of damage caused by cyberattacks.

Additionally, AI models can adapt to attacker changes in real-time. For instance, if an adversary modifies a malware payload to evade detection, an AI model trained on behavioral indicators not just static signatures can still flag the anomalous activity. This adaptive capability is essential in environments where threats mutate quickly and unpredictably.

The Future of Threat Intelligence

As cybercriminals increasingly leverage AI for offensive purposes such as using generative models to create polymorphic malware or launching automated phishing campaigns defenders must match this sophistication with equally advanced AI-powered tools. The future of threat intelligence lies in fully autonomous, self-learning systems that not only detect and analyze threats but also anticipate attacker moves, simulate counterattacks, and provide decision support in near real-time.

Furthermore, the integration of AI-driven threat intelligence with other domains such as fraud detection, insider threat monitoring, and national cyber defense will create a more holistic and resilient cybersecurity ecosystem. Multimodal AI systems that combine text, image, and behavioral data analysis will offer even deeper insights into emerging threats across diverse digital environments.

AI-driven threat intelligence frameworks represent a paradigm shift in cybersecurity, enabling organizations to move from reactive defense to proactive threat anticipation and mitigation. By leveraging machine learning, NLP, and automation, these frameworks transform raw data into actionable intelligence with speed and precision. They not only improve detection and response but also foster greater collaboration, informed decision-making, and resilience in the face of evolving cyber threats. As cyberattacks grow more intelligent and coordinated, AI-driven threat intelligence is not just an option it is an imperative for any organization committed to safeguarding its digital future.

B. Incident Response and Threat Mitigation Strategies

Effective incident response is a cornerstone of modern cybersecurity, especially as organizations face increasingly complex and targeted cyber threats. While prevention is ideal, the inevitability of security breaches underscores the critical need for well-structured incident response and threat mitigation strategies. These strategies not only limit the impact of cyber incidents but also help organizations recover swiftly, preserve digital evidence, and strengthen future defenses.

Incident response refers to the systematic approach an organization takes when identifying, managing, and resolving security breaches or attacks. This process is not a single event but a continuous cycle that involves preparation, detection, analysis, containment, eradication, recovery, and post-incident review. Each phase plays a vital role in minimizing damage and restoring normal operations.

Preparation begins long before an incident occurs. It involves establishing policies, assembling response teams, defining communication protocols, and ensuring that all personnel understand their roles. This phase also includes deploying technologies like intrusion detection systems (IDS), security information and event management (SIEM) platforms, and endpoint detection tools to facilitate early threat recognition.

Once a potential threat is detected, organizations must quickly analyze the scope and nature of the incident. Rapid detection and accurate classification whether the issue is a malware infection, data breach, insider threat, or DDoS attack allow the response team to take appropriate actions. During this phase, real-time threat intelligence and machine learning can accelerate identification, enabling automated alerts and prioritization based on threat severity.

Containment is crucial to prevent the threat from spreading across systems or networks. Depending on the severity and type of incident, this could involve isolating affected devices, shutting down compromised accounts, or segmenting parts of the network. Short-term containment is focused on immediate control, while long-term containment ensures that backdoors or persistent threats are neutralized.

After containing the threat, eradication involves removing the root cause of the incident. This could mean deleting malicious code, closing exploited vulnerabilities, patching systems, or reconfiguring firewalls and access controls. Thorough system scanning, forensic analysis, and validation are essential to confirm that the environment is clean and stable.

The recovery phase focuses on restoring affected systems and services to operational status. This involves re-imaging devices, restoring backups, validating system integrity, and continuously monitoring for signs of residual threat activity. Recovery efforts must be carefully timed and executed to avoid reintroducing vulnerabilities or triggering additional threats.

Post-incident review is perhaps the most undervalued but essential component of the response cycle. After resolving the incident, organizations should conduct a comprehensive analysis to identify what went wrong, how the incident was handled, and what improvements are needed. Lessons learned during this phase inform updates to security policies, training programs, and infrastructure investments, ultimately enhancing the organization's overall security posture.

Threat mitigation strategies extend beyond incident response. Proactive measures are necessary to reduce the risk of future incidents. This includes implementing zero trust principles, conducting regular security audits, and ensuring patch management processes are up to date. Organizations must also adopt strong identity and access management (IAM) controls, enforce multi-factor authentication (MFA), and encrypt sensitive data at rest and in transit.

Training employees to recognize phishing attempts, social engineering tactics, and suspicious behavior plays a key role in early threat detection. Human error remains one of the leading causes of breaches, and awareness programs can drastically reduce that risk. Similarly, tabletop exercises and simulated attacks help teams rehearse response scenarios and improve coordination under pressure.

AI-driven threat mitigation is also gaining traction. Predictive analytics, behavior-based anomaly detection, and automated response tools enable faster identification and remediation of threats. These technologies reduce the burden on human analysts and ensure that threats are addressed with speed and precision, even in large-scale or multi-vector attacks.

Collaboration is another pillar of effective threat mitigation. Sharing incident data, threat indicators, and remediation techniques with industry peers, government agencies, and cybersecurity communities contributes to collective defense. Platforms like threat intelligence sharing networks (e.g., ISACs) allow organizations to stay ahead of emerging threats and leverage collective expertise to respond faster and more effectively.

Ultimately, incident response and threat mitigation must be treated as continuous, evolving disciplines. Cyber adversaries are constantly adapting their tactics, so defense mechanisms must evolve in parallel. A robust response strategy is not only reactive but also preventive and adaptive capable of learning from past incidents, anticipating future threats, and reinforcing organizational resilience.

By investing in comprehensive response capabilities and forward-looking mitigation strategies, organizations can move beyond mere survival in the face of cyberattacks. They can become resilient entities capable of withstanding disruptions, protecting critical assets, and maintaining trust in a world where digital threats are an ever-present reality.

C. Penetration Testing and Vulnerability Assessments

Penetration testing and vulnerability assessments are fundamental components of a proactive cybersecurity strategy, designed to uncover weaknesses before adversaries can exploit them. These practices serve as the digital equivalent of a stress test, identifying exploitable points in an organization's infrastructure, applications, and network configurations. When executed effectively, they not only enhance an organization's security posture but also serve as a roadmap for continuous improvement, guiding the development of robust defense mechanisms and informed risk management strategies.

Penetration testing, often referred to as "ethical hacking," involves simulating real-world cyberattacks under controlled conditions to evaluate how well systems withstand various threat scenarios. Unlike automated scans, penetration tests are typically manual, tailored, and adaptive. Ethical hackers mimic the tactics, techniques, and procedures (TTPs) of malicious actors to assess how far they can infiltrate a system, what data they can access, and how long they can remain undetected. The goal is to identify critical security flaws such as misconfigurations, unpatched vulnerabilities, insecure protocols, and weak authentication systems that may not be visible through conventional security audits.

On the other hand, vulnerability assessments focus on systematically scanning systems, applications, and networks for known vulnerabilities. These assessments leverage automated tools to compare assets against a comprehensive database of documented weaknesses such as those listed in the Common Vulnerabilities and Exposures (CVE) repository. While penetration tests evaluate how a vulnerability might be exploited, vulnerability assessments prioritize and categorize security risks based on severity, exposure, and potential impact. Together, these approaches provide a comprehensive understanding of an organization's attack surface.

Integrating artificial intelligence (AI) into penetration testing and vulnerability assessments significantly enhances their efficacy. AI can automate reconnaissance processes, such as scanning ports, fingerprinting devices, and mapping network topologies. Machine learning models can analyze historical attack data to predict which vulnerabilities are most likely to be targeted by attackers. In real-time, AI systems can correlate threat intelligence with internal vulnerability data, offering more accurate prioritization of remediation efforts based on the threat landscape's dynamic nature.

In modern security operations, AI-driven penetration testing platforms are increasingly capable of autonomously identifying exploitable paths, executing attack chains, and recommending fixes. This shift reduces the burden on security teams while ensuring thorough coverage. Moreover, by incorporating AI-based behavioral analytics, penetration testers can simulate insider threats and advanced persistent threat (APT) tactics with greater precision, thereby testing not just perimeter defenses, but also internal security controls and user behavior monitoring systems.

Vulnerability assessments also benefit from AI's capacity to continuously scan large-scale, complex environments, flagging not only known vulnerabilities but also configuration anomalies and deviations from baseline security standards. Natural language processing (NLP) tools can parse unstructured security advisories and threat feeds to uncover emerging vulnerabilities and integrate them into scanning protocols swiftly.

To ensure effectiveness, both penetration testing and vulnerability assessments should be conducted regularly and integrated into the organization's broader risk management framework. Scheduled and unscheduled tests, red teaming exercises, and automated continuous scanning should coexist with manual assessments to achieve optimal visibility. The findings must feed into actionable reporting that translates technical details into executive-level insights, helping decision-makers allocate resources appropriately and align security investments with business objectives.

Additionally, regulatory requirements such as PCI DSS, HIPAA, and ISO 27001 increasingly mandate routine vulnerability assessments and penetration testing, making them essential not only for security but also for compliance. Incorporating these assessments into DevSecOps pipelines and continuous integration/continuous deployment (CI/CD) environments ensures that vulnerabilities are caught early in the development lifecycle, reducing remediation costs and accelerating time-to-market without compromising security.

Penetration testing and vulnerability assessments are indispensable tools in the cybersecurity arsenal. When enhanced by AI and aligned with strategic goals, they evolve from reactive checklists to dynamic instruments of threat anticipation, risk reduction, and digital resilience. Organizations that prioritize and continuously refine these practices stand better equipped to defend their assets, safeguard their data, and maintain stakeholder trust in an increasingly hostile digital landscape.

CHAPTER SIX

Cloud and IoT Security in Forensic Investigations

The rapid proliferation of cloud computing and the Internet of Things (IoT) has revolutionized modern digital ecosystems, offering unprecedented scalability, connectivity, and operational efficiency. However, these same technologies have also expanded the attack surface, presenting new and complex challenges for forensic investigators. In an era where data is decentralized, transient, and highly distributed, traditional forensic approaches must be reimagined to address the dynamic nature of cloud environments and IoT infrastructures. This chapter explores the evolving strategies and methodologies used to conduct forensic investigations within these technologically advanced domains.

Cloud forensics involves the identification, preservation, analysis, and presentation of digital evidence stored across virtualized environments. Unlike traditional computing systems, where investigators have physical access to hard drives and network equipment, cloud platforms often operate under shared responsibility models, complicating access and jurisdictional boundaries. Forensic investigators must collaborate closely with cloud service providers (CSPs) to obtain metadata, access logs, and system snapshots, all while ensuring the chain of custody is preserved and evidence integrity remains intact.

One of the primary challenges in cloud forensics is the volatility of data. Cloud environments rely on real-time resource allocation, and virtual machines can be spun up and decommissioned within minutes. Logs may be overwritten or deleted based on retention policies, and encryption mechanisms can prevent unauthorized access even to investigators. These variables necessitate rapid incident response capabilities and automated tools capturing evidence immediately upon detection of a breach. Moreover, forensic readiness planning, including predefined data retention strategies and audit logging configurations, must be embedded into cloud security architecture from the outset.

AI and machine learning technologies are instrumental in navigating the complexities of cloud forensics. Intelligent algorithms can sift through massive volumes of data to detect anomalies, correlate events, and uncover the root causes of security incidents. Behavioral analytics can differentiate between legitimate administrative activities and suspicious behavior, reducing false positives and expediting investigative timelines. Furthermore, AI-driven log analysis tools can reconstruct timelines of attacker activity across multi-cloud and hybrid environments, revealing the path of intrusion and the scope of impact.

IoT forensics presents another unique set of challenges. IoT devices from smart thermostats to industrial sensors often operate with limited processing power, storage capacity, and built-in security controls. These constraints hinder traditional forensic techniques, as logs may be minimal or entirely absent, and data might be stored in proprietary formats or transmitted to remote servers. Additionally, IoT devices are highly heterogeneous, with varying communication protocols, firmware architectures, and update mechanisms. As such, forensic investigations must adopt a flexible and adaptive framework tailored to each device type and usage context.

Security breaches involving IoT devices can have far-reaching implications, especially in critical infrastructure sectors such as healthcare, transportation, and energy. Investigators must not only analyze the compromised device but also trace communications across the network to identify command-and-control servers, lateral movement patterns, and secondary payloads. Packet sniffing, radio frequency (RF) analysis, and firmware reverse engineering have become essential tools in uncovering hidden threats and validating the integrity of IoT systems.

Cloud and IoT forensics also intersect in smart environments, where sensor data, cloud analytics, and automated decision-making converge. In such settings, forensic investigators must be able to trace data lineage from the point of capture on an IoT device, through cloud-based processing systems, to the final output. Blockchain technology is increasingly being explored as a solution for maintaining immutable logs and data provenance across distributed systems, providing additional assurance in legal proceedings.

Legal and compliance considerations are equally critical in cloud and IoT forensics. Investigators must navigate issues such as data sovereignty, cross-border evidence handling, and multi-tenant data isolation. Ensuring that investigations comply with regulations such as the General Data Protection Regulation (GDPR) and the California Consumer Privacy Act (CCPA) requires a thorough understanding of legal frameworks and close coordination with legal counsel and cloud vendors.

To address these complexities, organizations must adopt a proactive approach to forensic readiness. This includes implementing logging and monitoring solutions tailored to cloud and IoT systems, training staff in specialized investigation techniques, and maintaining updated incident response playbooks. Security teams should also conduct regular forensic drills to test their readiness and adapt to emerging threats.

In conclusion, as the digital world becomes increasingly interconnected and reliant on cloud and IoT technologies, forensic investigations must evolve to keep pace. By leveraging AI, developing specialized tools, and fostering cross-disciplinary collaboration, investigators can uncover digital evidence even in the most challenging environments. The future of cyber forensics depends on our ability to navigate these complex ecosystems with precision, adaptability, and foresight ensuring that justice and accountability remain achievable in an ever-shifting technological landscape.

A. Investigating Cyber Threats in Cloud Environments

As organizations increasingly migrate their operations to cloud infrastructures, the complexity and scale of cyber threats targeting these environments have grown exponentially. Investigating cyber threats in cloud environments demands a fundamentally different approach from traditional on-premises forensics. It requires an understanding of distributed architectures, virtualized systems, and shared responsibility models, all of which redefine how evidence is collected, preserved, and analyzed.

Cloud environments are dynamic, elastic, and often decentralized, which introduces unique challenges in identifying the source and impact of cyber threats. Unlike traditional systems where data resides on physical hardware within a single organization's control, cloud services span multiple data centers, geographical regions, and service layers. As a result, investigators must navigate issues related to data sovereignty, access restrictions, and provider-specific logging structures.

One of the primary challenges in cloud forensics is visibility. Cloud service providers (CSPs) often maintain control over the underlying infrastructure, leaving customers with limited access to system-level logs and metadata. To address this, investigators must rely on cloud-native tools and APIs to retrieve relevant data, such as user activity logs, virtual machine snapshots, storage access records, and network flow logs. Tools like AWS CloudTrail, Microsoft Azure Monitor, and Google Cloud's operations suite have become essential in facilitating this level of visibility.

Another critical factor is the ephemeral nature of cloud assets. Instances can be spun up and terminated within minutes, making it difficult to capture and preserve volatile data. Investigators must act swiftly to collect evidence before it is overwritten or lost. Automation plays a significant role here, enabling continuous monitoring and immediate alerting suspicious behavior that warrants deeper forensic analysis.

The shared responsibility model adds another layer of complexity. While CSPs are responsible for securing the infrastructure, customers are accountable for securing their data, applications, and access controls. This dual responsibility means that investigators must understand both the cloud provider's security mechanisms and the customer's configuration to determine how a breach occurred. Misconfigurations such as exposed storage buckets or improperly secured APIs remain among the most common entry points for attackers.

In cloud environments, threats often manifest through credential theft, privilege escalation, lateral movement across virtual networks, and exploitation of insecure APIs. Forensic investigations in these scenarios involve tracing access logs, examining identity and access management (IAM) policies, and mapping the attacker's path through the environment.

The goal is to reconstruct the timeline of the intrusion, identify the methods used, and assess the scope of the compromise.

Encryption adds another dimension to cloud investigations. While encryption is vital for protecting data, it can complicate forensic efforts if decryption keys are inaccessible or if encrypted communications obscure malicious activities. Investigators must ensure that appropriate key management practices are in place and that they have lawful access to encrypted data during investigations.

Multi-tenancy in cloud platforms also raises concerns about evidence segregation and data contamination. Forensic processes must be meticulously designed to isolate an organization's data from that of other tenants to avoid legal and ethical violations. This requires close collaboration with CSPs and, in some cases, adherence to court-approved processes and chain-of-custody documentation to ensure evidentiary integrity.

To support investigations in cloud environments, many organizations now incorporate security orchestration, automation, and response (SOAR) platforms alongside cloud security posture management (CSPM) tools. These technologies provide a centralized view of security configurations, automate threat detection and response, and streamline the collection of forensic artifacts across cloud platforms.

Incident response teams must also be equipped with specialized training to interpret cloud-specific telemetry and understand the nuances of different service models Infrastructure as a Service (IaaS), Platform as a Service (PaaS), and Software as a Service (SaaS). Each model presents unique forensic challenges and requires tailored investigative techniques.

Ultimately, effective cyber threat investigation in cloud environments hinges on preparedness, collaboration, and the use of advanced tools. Organizations must establish clear protocols for cloud incident response, define roles and responsibilities, and maintain strong partnerships with their cloud providers. Regular audits, proactive monitoring, and threat hunting in the cloud environment are essential for early detection and effective response.

As the cloud becomes the new digital frontier, the ability to investigate and respond to cyber threats within it is no longer optional. Mastery of cloud forensics ensures that organizations can maintain trust, recover from breaches swiftly, and continue operating securely in a landscape defined by agility, scale, and innovation.

B. IoT Forensics: Challenges and Emerging Solutions

The rise of the Internet of Things (IoT) has ushered in a new era of hyperconnectivity, enabling smart homes, intelligent transportation systems, and industrial automation. However, with this interconnectedness comes a significant increase in potential vulnerabilities. From smart refrigerators to wearable health devices and industrial control systems, IoT ecosystems are vast, diverse, and often lack standardized security measures. This has posed formidable challenges for digital forensic investigators, who are now faced with the daunting task of collecting, analyzing, and preserving evidence across a fragmented and often volatile landscape.

One of the most pressing challenges in IoT forensics is the heterogeneity of devices and platforms. IoT devices vary widely in terms of hardware architecture, operating systems, firmware, and communication protocols. Many are designed with limited storage and processing power, leaving little room for detailed logging or forensic data collection. Moreover, proprietary technologies and closed-source designs frequently restrict access to internal device data, hindering forensic analysis. Investigators must navigate a patchwork of device-specific procedures, often reverse-engineering hardware or software just to retrieve relevant evidence.

Data volatility is another critical issue. IoT devices are often designed for real-time data transmission, with minimal or no local storage. Information may be ephemeral transmitted to the cloud and immediately deleted from the device making evidence collection highly time sensitive. Additionally, logs may be overwritten frequently due to constrained memory capacities, and standard timestamping mechanisms may be absent, complicating timeline reconstruction.

Device accessibility and physical constraints also play a role. IoT devices are frequently embedded in difficult-to-reach locations within machinery, walls, or wearable gear. Physical access for evidence acquisition may be impractical or impossible without damaging the device. Some devices also lack standard interfaces (such as USB ports or JTAG connectors), requiring advanced techniques like chip-off forensics to extract data directly from memory chips.

Security limitations in IoT design further complicate forensic efforts. Many IoT devices are shipped with default credentials, outdated firmware, or no encryption, making them easy targets for attackers and also raising concerns about evidence integrity. Without robust authentication and encryption, forensic investigators must take extra steps to verify that data has not been tampered with, whether by malicious actors or during the collection process.

Despite these challenges, emerging solutions are beginning to reshape the landscape of IoT forensics. Standardization efforts are underway, with industry bodies advocating for baseline security and logging requirements in IoT product development. These initiatives aim to make devices more forensic-friendly by mandating secure audit trails, timestamping, and secure storage of event data. Moreover, open-source forensic toolkits tailored for IoT environments are gaining traction, offering modular frameworks for parsing logs, capturing network traffic, and analyzing firmware across a range of devices.

AI and machine learning are also playing a pivotal role in overcoming IoT forensic hurdles. Automated anomaly detection systems can monitor large fleets of IoT devices for deviations from normal behavior, flagging potential compromises in real time. Machine learning algorithms can help correlate activity across distributed sensor networks, identify patterns, and reconstruct events even when direct logs are missing or incomplete. This intelligent inference approach enhances the speed and accuracy of forensic investigations.

Cloud-integrated forensics provides another promising avenue. Since many IoT devices offload data to the cloud, forensic investigators can access more persistent records from cloud logs, analytics platforms, and remote databases. Collaboration with cloud service providers can yield valuable insights into device behavior, user interactions, and environmental context, significantly enriching the evidentiary record.

To build resilience in IoT ecosystems, organizations are increasingly adopting forensic-by-design approaches. This involves integrating forensic readiness into the device development lifecycle, from hardware and firmware design to cloud integration. By embedding features such as secure logging, remote evidence retrieval, and immutable audit trails, manufacturers can ensure their products support post-incident investigations without compromising operational performance.

While IoT forensics presents complex and evolving challenges, it also offers fertile ground for innovation. Through cross-disciplinary collaboration, technological advancement, and proactive system design, the forensic community can adapt to the unique demands of the IoT era. As our reliance on interconnected devices deepens, robust forensic capabilities will be essential for maintaining trust, accountability, and security across the digital frontier.

C. AI's Role in Securing Decentralized Digital Ecosystems

The expansion of decentralized digital ecosystems, encompassing blockchain networks, peer-to-peer architectures, and distributed IoT systems, has redefined how data is managed, stored, and exchanged across cyberspace. While decentralization promotes autonomy, transparency, and resilience, it simultaneously introduces new layers of complexity and vulnerability that traditional cybersecurity mechanisms struggle to address. In this context, artificial intelligence (AI) has emerged as a transformative force enabling dynamic security, intelligent threat detection, and adaptive risk management within decentralized environments.

Decentralized ecosystems lack a central authority or control node, which means security enforcement and incident response must also be distributed. AI plays a critical role by providing autonomous decision-making capabilities that allow individual nodes or endpoints to detect anomalies, verify integrity, and respond to potential breaches in real-time. Machine learning algorithms can continuously monitor network behavior, identifying patterns that deviate from established norms whether it be unauthorized access, unusual transaction flows, or compromised device behavior without relying on a central monitoring system.

In blockchain-based systems, AI enhances security by analyzing smart contract behavior and consensus mechanisms for anomalies and vulnerabilities. Given that smart contracts are immutable once deployed, flaws can have irreversible consequences. AI-driven tools can perform code audits, simulate attack scenarios, and highlight potential logical or operational flaws before deployment. Additionally, natural language processing (NLP) algorithms can parse and analyze decentralized communications, ensuring that coordination within these ecosystems adheres to security protocols and compliance requirements.

AI is also instrumental in automating threat intelligence across decentralized networks. In such architectures, threat data is often fragmented across nodes. AI consolidates this fragmented data, extracts meaningful insights, and disseminates actionable intelligence in real time. This distributed threat intelligence model allows ecosystems to respond proactively isolating threats, initiating patches, and updating security policies autonomously across nodes.

Another key contribution of AI is in identity verification and trust management within decentralized digital systems. In environments where traditional identity and access control frameworks do not apply, AI facilitates the creation of behavioral biometrics and trust scoring models. These models assess user and device behavior over time, building adaptive trust profiles that are used to validate interactions, detect impersonation, and restrict access when suspicious patterns emerge.

Moreover, AI strengthens data integrity and consensus validation. In decentralized systems, especially those reliant on consensus algorithms like proof-of-work or proof-of-stake, anomalies in transaction validation can compromise system reliability. AI-powered validators can analyze transaction trends, flag inconsistencies, and improve consensus accuracy ensuring that only legitimate actions are recorded and propagated across the network.

AI's real-time responsiveness is particularly useful in securing edge computing and fog networks, where data processing occurs closer to the source. These environments often underpin IoT and smart infrastructure solutions. By deploying lightweight AI models at the edge, decentralized ecosystems can autonomously filter threats, perform local analysis, and protect sensitive operations without needing constant connectivity to a centralized data center.

Despite these advances, integrating AI into decentralized systems is not without challenges. The lack of centralized training data, data privacy concerns, and the complexity of deploying machine learning models across heterogeneous nodes all present ongoing barriers. However, techniques such as federated learning, where AI models are trained collaboratively without sharing raw data, offer promising paths forward ensuring both privacy and performance.

In essence, the integration of AI into decentralized digital ecosystems marks a significant leap forward in cybersecurity resilience. It enables distributed networks to operate with greater autonomy, adaptiveness, and intelligence, transforming them from passive systems into proactive defenders. As digital infrastructure continues to decentralize, AI will be indispensable in shaping secure, self-sustaining ecosystems capable of resisting sophisticated cyber threats in real time.

CHAPTER SEVEN

Digital Risk Management and Cyber Resilience

As organizations face an increasing array of cyber threats; the importance of robust digital risk management and cyber resilience has never been more evident. The sophistication of modern cybercrime, coupled with the complexity of global digital infrastructures, demands that businesses take a proactive approach to identifying, mitigating, and responding to digital risks. This chapter delves into the principles and practices of digital risk management, exploring how organizations can strengthen their cybersecurity posture, safeguard critical assets, and ensure operational continuity in the face of cyber incidents.

Understanding Digital Risk Management

Digital risk management is a comprehensive strategy aimed at protecting an organization's digital assets and ensuring its resilience against cyber threats. It involves identifying potential risks, evaluating their impact, and implementing preventive measures to reduce vulnerabilities. In today's interconnected world, digital risk management is not confined to IT departments alone. It spans the entire organization, requiring collaboration between business leaders, cybersecurity experts, and operational teams to develop a holistic approach to risk mitigation.

Key components of digital risk management include asset identification, risk assessment, and incident response planning. A crucial first step is identifying critical assets such as intellectual property, customer data, financial systems, and network infrastructures. Once these assets are cataloged, organizations can assess the potential risks they face, including data breaches, cyber-attacks, and system failures. Risk assessments also involve evaluating the likelihood and potential consequences of various threats, allowing businesses to prioritize their efforts and allocate resources effectively.

The Importance of Cyber Resilience

Cyber resilience goes beyond traditional cybersecurity measures by emphasizing the ability of an organization to adapt and recover from cyber incidents. Unlike conventional risk management, which focuses on preventing attacks, cyber resilience takes a more comprehensive view of an organization's ability to absorb, withstand, and recover from cyber threats without significant disruption to business operations.

Building cyber resilience requires organizations to develop strategies for continuous monitoring, rapid response, and recovery. This includes having real-time threat detection systems in place, conducting regular security audits, and implementing incident response protocols that can be quickly activated in the event of a breach. A resilient organization can quickly detect anomalies, contain threats, and minimize damage, ensuring that it can continue to function even in the aftermath of a cyberattack.

Integrating AI and Machine Learning into Risk Management

The integration of artificial intelligence (AI) and machine learning (ML) into digital risk management has revolutionized how organizations detect and mitigate cyber risks. These technologies enable automated risk assessments, predictive threat detection, and enhanced decision-making. AI-powered systems can analyze vast amounts of data, identify patterns, and detect anomalies that would otherwise go unnoticed by traditional methods. This not only enhances the speed and accuracy of risk identification but also enables organizations to respond to threats proactively rather than reactively.

AI-driven systems can continuously monitor network traffic, detect malware, and identify emerging threats in real time. Machine learning algorithms can be trained to recognize the characteristics of known attack vectors, enabling systems to anticipate and defend against cyber threats before they manifest. The dynamic nature of AI also allows these systems to adapt to evolving threat landscapes, ensuring that risk management protocols remain up to date in the face of new and sophisticated attacks.

Developing a Cyber Resilience Framework

Creating a resilient cybersecurity framework involves several key steps that work together to protect an organization from cyber risks. One of the most important elements is the establishment of a security governance structure that aligns with business goals and regulatory requirements. Security leaders must collaborate with executive management to ensure that cybersecurity is treated as a strategic priority and integrated into the broader risk management framework.

Another essential component is the implementation of strong identity and access management (IAM) protocols. Effective IAM ensures that only authorized users can access sensitive systems and data, reducing the risk of insider threats and unauthorized access. Multi-factor authentication (MFA), strong encryption standards, and regular user access reviews are essential in maintaining a secure environment.

Regular risk assessments, vulnerability management, and penetration testing are crucial practices for identifying weaknesses within an organization's infrastructure. By simulating real-world attack scenarios, organizations can identify gaps in their security measures and improve their defenses. A proactive approach to vulnerability management ensures that organizations stay one step ahead of potential cybercriminals.

Finally, businesses should ensure that they have a robust incident response plan (IRP) in place. An effective IRP outlines the steps to take in the event of a cyberattack, from containment to recovery. It is crucial that this plan is regularly tested and updated, so that employees know how to react quickly and efficiently when an incident occurs.

The Role of Cybersecurity Professionals in Digital Risk Management

Cybersecurity professionals play a central role in the development and execution of digital risk management strategies. These experts are responsible for assessing the organization's digital risk landscape, recommending appropriate security measures, and leading the implementation of cybersecurity policies. They are also the first line of defense when it comes to identifying, containing, and neutralizing cyber threats.

Cybersecurity professionals must be equipped with the latest knowledge and tools to tackle new and emerging threats. Ongoing training and certification programs are essential to ensure that they are well-versed in the latest trends, technologies, and best practices. As organizations continue to embrace digital transformation, the role of cybersecurity professionals in managing digital risks will become even more critical.

Case Study: Enhancing Cyber Resilience in Financial Institutions

A key example of successful digital risk management can be seen in the financial sector. Given the high value of financial data and the sophistication of cyber threats targeting financial institutions, these organizations have been at the forefront of implementing comprehensive cyber resilience strategies.

One prominent financial institution implemented an AI-driven risk assessment platform that continuously monitored transaction data and user behavior patterns. This system was able to detect fraudulent activities in real-time, minimizing the risk of financial losses and reputation damage. Additionally, the institution conducted regular penetration testing and vulnerability assessments, ensuring that its digital infrastructure was resilient to attacks.

By integrating AI-powered solutions into their risk management strategies, financial institutions have been able to achieve a higher level of operational continuity, even in the face of sophisticated cyber threats. This approach not only protected critical data but also enhanced customer trust, which is vital in the competitive world of finance.

The Future of Digital Risk Management and Cyber Resilience

Looking ahead, digital risk management and cyber resilience will become even more intertwined as organizations continue to embrace AI, cloud computing, and IoT technologies. As these technologies evolve, so too will the cyber threat landscape, requiring businesses to adapt and innovate continuously.

In the future, we can expect even more advanced AI and machine learning solutions for risk management and cyber resilience. These tools will be able to predict and prevent attacks with greater accuracy, while also offering enhanced automation to reduce the human error factor. Businesses will need to continue developing comprehensive cybersecurity frameworks, ensuring that they are prepared for new challenges and capable of defending against advanced cyber threats.

Moreover, the rise of decentralized systems, such as blockchain and cryptocurrency platforms, will present new challenges in managing digital risk. As these technologies become more integrated into the global economy, ensuring their security will be paramount in maintaining cyber resilience.

Digital risk management and cyber resilience are critical to the future of cybersecurity. Organizations that embrace these strategies will be better equipped to handle the complexities of modern cyber threats, safeguard their assets, and ensure business continuity in an increasingly hostile digital environment. With the right tools, technologies, and mindset, businesses can not only protect themselves from cyber risks but also build a foundation for long-term success and resilience in the digital age.

A. AI-Based Risk Assessment and Management Models

In the rapidly evolving digital landscape, the growing sophistication of cyber threats requires organizations to adopt more advanced and proactive strategies to protect their assets, data, and systems. Artificial intelligence (AI) has become a game-changer in the realm of risk assessment and management, providing enhanced capabilities for identifying, evaluating, and mitigating potential threats. AI-based risk assessment models enable organizations to go beyond traditional, static approaches, allowing for dynamic, real-time evaluation of risks and more precise decision-making in response to emerging security challenges.

At the heart of AI-driven risk management is the ability to analyze vast amounts of data from diverse sources and identify patterns that may otherwise go unnoticed. Traditional risk assessment models often rely on predefined criteria and historical data, which may not fully capture the complexity and fluidity of modern cyber threats. In contrast, AI-based models leverage machine learning algorithms, deep learning techniques, and data mining to continually learn from new data, adapting and improving their risk assessments over time. This constant evolution allows organizations to stay ahead of evolving attack methods and to better anticipate potential vulnerabilities before they are exploited.

One of the primary advantages of AI in risk assessment is its ability to perform predictive analysis. By analyzing historical data and identifying correlations between past incidents and current threat landscapes, AI systems can forecast the likelihood of certain types of attacks occurring in the future. These predictive models help organizations assess the probability of a risk materializing and prioritizing their mitigation efforts accordingly. For example, an AI system might predict an increased risk of a phishing attack based on current trends, such as a rise in targeted social engineering campaigns or specific geopolitical events, allowing the organization to bolster its defenses ahead of time.

AI can also significantly improve anomaly detection a critical component of risk management. Rather than relying solely on predefined rules or known attack signatures, AI-based systems can detect abnormal behavior across networks, devices, and applications. By analyzing user activity, traffic patterns, and system interactions, AI systems can identify deviations from typical behavior, flagging potential security breaches in real-time. This proactive detection allows organizations to respond to threats faster, often preventing attacks before they escalate into serious incidents. For example, an AI system might detect unusual patterns of data access or login attempts and immediately trigger an investigation into potential insider threats or external compromises.

In addition to anomaly detection, AI-driven risk management models excel in automating the risk mitigation process. Once a potential risk is identified, AI systems can take immediate, predefined actions to minimize exposure. These actions might include isolating compromised systems, block suspicious network traffic, or enforce additional authentication measures for high-risk operations. By automating these responses, organizations can mitigate risks without the need for constant human intervention, ensuring faster and more efficient incident resolution.

Another key aspect of AI-based risk management is dynamic risk scoring, which adjusts in real-time based on continuously updated data. Traditional risk assessments typically assign static risk scores based on historical data and predefined factors. However, in a fast-paced and ever-changing threat landscape, this approach can quickly become outdated. AI-powered models, on the other hand, continuously analyze a wide array of factors such as emerging threat intelligence, environmental context, and system vulnerabilities to dynamically adjust risk scores and prioritize remediation efforts accordingly. This real-time risk scoring helps organizations focus their resources on the most pressing threats, rather than being overwhelmed by an endless list of potential risks.

AI also plays a vital role in improving incident response and recovery. After a cybersecurity incident, AI-based systems can analyze the attack's impact and recommend actions for recovery. By examining the scope of the attack, affected systems, and compromised data, AI can help organizations restore normal operations while minimizing further damage. For example, AI systems can assist in determining the best path for system recovery, such as rolling back to a known safe state or applying automated patches to address vulnerabilities exploited during the attack.

One of the most promising applications of AI in risk management is in continuous monitoring and adaptive defense. Traditional risk management approaches often involve periodic assessments and scheduled reviews, but these methods may not be sufficient in addressing the constant and evolving nature of cyber threats. AI, however, enables continuous monitoring of digital infrastructures, providing real-time assessments of risks and vulnerabilities. By integrating AI into their security infrastructure, organizations can ensure that risk assessments and threat mitigation strategies are always up to date, adapting instantly to new developments or tactics used by cybercriminals.

As AI-powered risk management models become more sophisticated, they will increasingly be integrated into integrated cybersecurity frameworks. These frameworks combine risk assessment, detection, response, and recovery into a unified, automated system that offers end-to-end protection. AI can enhance these frameworks by analyzing data from multiple security tools, correlating events, and providing a holistic view of the organization's risk posture. This integration enables cybersecurity teams to make more informed decisions, deploy more effective countermeasures, and proactively defend against future threats.

AI-based risk assessment and management models represent a fundamental shift in the way organizations approach cybersecurity. By utilizing the power of machine learning, predictive analysis, anomaly detection, and automation, AI enables organizations to move beyond reactive measures and proactively manage risk in an increasingly complex digital environment. As the cybersecurity landscape continues to evolve, AI-driven solutions will become indispensable in safeguarding organizations against a broad array of cyber threats, ensuring the resilience and security of their digital infrastructures.

B. Preventive Security Measures and Incident Response Planning

Preventive security measures and incident response planning are integral components of a robust cybersecurity strategy. As organizations face increasing cyber threats, it is crucial to establish proactive measures that not only prevent security breaches but also prepare teams for rapid and effective responses in the event of an incident.

Preventive security measures involve creating layers of defense across the entire infrastructure, reducing the potential for cybercriminals to exploit vulnerabilities. This includes a combination of technical controls, organizational policies, and employee awareness training. Implementing multifactor authentication (MFA), encryption protocols, and regular security patching schedules are foundational actions that protect sensitive data and systems from external and internal threats. Furthermore, cybersecurity frameworks such as NIST, ISO 27001, and CIS Controls provide guidelines for organizations to structure their security posture and minimize risks.

A key aspect of preventive security is continuous monitoring and risk assessment. Through security information and event management (SIEM) systems, threat intelligence platforms, and behavior analytics, organizations can track suspicious activities and detect anomalies in real-time. Additionally, regularly conducting penetration tests and vulnerability assessments helps identify potential weaknesses before attackers can exploit them.

However, no preventive measure is foolproof, which is why incident response planning is essential. An effective incident response (IR) plan ensures that an organization can quickly and efficiently manage a cybersecurity incident, minimizing its impact and reducing recovery time. The response process involves identifying, containing, eradicating, and recovering from an attack. A well-prepared incident response team can also mitigate reputational damage and legal ramifications by executing the plan promptly and maintaining communication with stakeholders.

An important part of an incident response plan is the post-incident analysis, which helps organizations understand the cause of the breach and take corrective actions. By learning from each incident, businesses can continuously improve their security posture, making them more resilient to future attacks. Developing a culture of preparedness, where employees are regularly trained on cybersecurity best practices and incident response protocols, further strengthens the organization's overall defense.

Ultimately, preventive security measures combined with a well-defined incident response plan create a comprehensive cybersecurity strategy. These efforts ensure that organizations are not only protected against potential cyber risks but are also prepared to handle incidents effectively, ensuring business continuity and resilience in the face of evolving cyber threats.

C. Strengthening Cyber Resilience Through Proactive Forensic Strategies

Strengthening cyber resilience through proactive forensic strategies is becoming increasingly vital as the complexity and frequency of cyberattacks continue to rise. In the past, cybersecurity efforts primarily focused on responding to incidents once they occurred. However, with the evolving nature of threats, this reactive approach is no longer sufficient. Organizations today must adopt a proactive stance to not only detect and mitigate threats but also to anticipate and neutralize them before they can cause significant damage.

Proactive forensic strategies begin with real-time monitoring and threat intelligence gathering. By utilizing advanced forensic tools, security teams can continuously monitor networks, endpoints, and systems for signs of suspicious activity. AI-driven detection algorithms can analyze vast amounts of data quickly, identifying potential threats that may go unnoticed by human analysts. This continuous vigilance enables early intervention, reducing the window of opportunity for cybercriminals to exploit vulnerabilities.

Another essential aspect of proactive forensic strategies is predictive analytics. By leveraging machine learning and AI-based models, security professionals can forecast potential attack patterns and identify vulnerabilities before they are targeted. This allows organizations to implement preventive measures, such as system hardening, patch management, and targeted employee training, to eliminate or minimize known risks. Predictive analytics can also guide the development of more effective incident response plans, ensuring that security teams are prepared for various threat scenarios.

Furthermore, strengthening cyber resilience requires an integrated approach across all organizational levels. From IT infrastructure to employee education, every aspect of an organization's security posture must be aligned to support proactive forensic strategies. This includes implementing regular security audits, penetration testing, and vulnerability assessments to uncover weaknesses before they are exploited. The ability to continuously assess and address vulnerabilities ensures that organizations remain agile and adaptable in the face of changing threats.

Proactive forensic strategies also emphasize the importance of collaboration across industries and sectors. By sharing threat intelligence and collaborating on best practices, organizations can strengthen their defenses collectively. Cybercriminals often operate in sophisticated cross-border networks, so building strong partnerships between private and public entities enhances overall security. Government agencies, law enforcement, and industry groups must work together to create a more resilient cybersecurity ecosystem.

Strengthening cyber resilience through proactive forensic strategies is not only about implementing advanced tools and technologies but also about fostering a security-first mindset throughout the organization. By continuously improving defenses, anticipating threats, and preparing for the unknown, businesses can stay ahead of cybercriminals and protect their digital assets. As cyber threats become increasingly sophisticated, proactive forensic strategies are key to ensuring that organizations are not just prepared for today's threats, but resilient against the challenges of tomorrow.

CHAPTER EIGHT

Challenges and Future Trends in Cyber Forensics

As the landscape of digital crime evolves, the field of cyber forensics faces both new challenges and exciting opportunities. While the tools and methodologies employed in cyber forensics continue to advance, numerous obstacles remain that complicate the process of investigating digital crimes. These challenges require the continued evolution of strategies, frameworks, and technologies to effectively combat increasingly sophisticated cyber threats. Moreover, the future of cyber forensics holds promising developments, especially with the integration of emerging technologies like Artificial Intelligence (AI), Machine Learning (ML), and blockchain, which are poised to reshape the way digital investigations are conducted.

One of the most significant challenges facing cyber forensics today is the sheer volume and complexity of data involved in modern cybercrime investigations. The proliferation of cloud services, Internet of Things (IoT) devices, and decentralized networks has exponentially increased the amount of digital evidence that investigators must process. This massive volume of data, combined with the need for timely analysis, places a strain on forensic investigators who must sift through terabytes of information to uncover relevant evidence. The growing diversity of data types, including encrypted files, anonymized communication, and sophisticated attack methods like polymorphic malware, adds layers of complexity to investigations, making it difficult to detect and attribute cybercrimes accurately.

A second critical challenge in cyber forensics is the fast-evolving nature of cybercrime itself. Cybercriminals are continually adapting and innovating their tactics, techniques, and procedures (TTPs) to evade detection. Whether through the use of advanced encryption, anonymous networks like Tor, or employing artificial intelligence to carry out highly automated attacks, cybercriminals are making it more difficult for forensics teams to track their activities. Additionally, the cross-border nature of cybercrime presents jurisdictional challenges, as crimes are often perpetrated across multiple countries, each with varying laws and regulations concerning digital forensics. The lack of international cooperation and the complexity of navigating diverse legal systems further complicates the efforts to bring perpetrators to justice.

Another pressing challenge is the rapid pace at which technology evolves. With new advancements in quantum computing, blockchain, and AI-driven cyberattacks, cyber forensics professionals are constantly playing catch-up. The ability to quickly adopt and integrate new technologies to stay ahead of cybercriminals is essential for the continued success of digital investigations. However, the lack of skilled professionals, combined with the high cost of training and acquiring state-of-the-art tools, presents a barrier to effective response in many organizations. The shortage of expertise in advanced forensic techniques, particularly in emerging technologies such as cloud forensics and IoT forensics, exacerbates the problem.

Despite these challenges, the future of cyber forensics holds immense promise, particularly with the integration of artificial intelligence and machine learning into forensic investigations. AI-powered tools can enhance the speed and accuracy of digital evidence analysis by automatically identifying patterns, anomalies, and correlations that may otherwise go unnoticed. This can drastically reduce the time required for evidence processing, enabling forensic investigators to focus on more complex aspects of the investigation. Moreover, predictive analytics powered by AI can be employed to proactively detect cybercrime activities before they occur, offering a more proactive approach to digital security.

Machine learning algorithms are also poised to enhance forensic investigations by automatically detecting and classifying malicious activity across large datasets. These algorithms can identify previously unknown attack methods by analyzing patterns and continuously learning from new data, thus improving the ability to identify threats in real time. In addition, machine learning can assist in the automation of repetitive tasks, such as data triage and preliminary analysis, allowing investigators to concentrate on higher-level decision-making and strategy.

Blockchain technology also has the potential to revolutionize digital forensics by providing an immutable and transparent way to track and verify digital evidence. Blockchain's decentralized ledger system could offer a secure and verifiable way to preserve digital evidence throughout the investigation process, reducing the risk of evidence tampering and enhancing the credibility of digital investigations in legal proceedings.

As digital environments become more interconnected, there will also be an increasing need for cross-discipline collaboration. Cyber forensics professionals will need to work closely with data scientists, legal experts, law enforcement agencies, and technology vendors to tackle the growing complexity of cybercrime. Collaborative efforts will be crucial in ensuring that forensic investigations can keep pace with the rapid changes in technology and the evolving tactics used by cybercriminals.

While the challenges facing cyber forensics are formidable, the future holds significant promise with the advent of advanced technologies and collaborative approaches. By integrating AI, machine learning, and blockchain into forensic practices, the cybersecurity community will be better equipped to combat cybercrime in the digital age. The continued development of skilled professionals and the implementation of innovative tools and strategies will be key to ensuring that cyber forensics remains a critical component of the global fight against digital crime. As technology advances, so too must the methods and capabilities of cyber forensics professionals, who must stay ahead of cybercriminals to maintain digital security and protect the integrity of evidence.

A. AI and Deepfake Threats to Digital Security

The rise of artificial intelligence (AI) and deep-fake technologies presents a significant challenge to digital security, creating new avenues for cybercriminals to exploit. While AI has revolutionized numerous industries, it also brings with it a host of cybersecurity concerns, particularly in the form of deepfakes hyper-realistic digital media that manipulates video, audio, and images to deceive viewers. This subheading explores the intersection of AI and deep-fake threats, examining the risks they pose to digital security, and how organizations can defend against them.

AI-powered deepfake technology has advanced to the point where it is increasingly difficult to distinguish between real and fabricated content. Deepfakes are not only a threat to personal privacy but also to businesses, governments, and even entire nations. Cybercriminals can use deepfakes to create fraudulent news reports, manipulate stock prices, or impersonate executives in video conferences, causing severe reputational damage and financial loss. Additionally, the use of deepfakes for social engineering attacks, such as voice phishing or "vishing," is on the rise. With a deepfake audio file that mimics an executive's voice, attackers can trick employees into transferring large sums of money or providing sensitive information, all while avoiding traditional authentication measures.

Deepfake technology also poses risks to political stability, as malicious actors can use it to create fake videos of politicians or public figures making controversial statements, leading to misinformation campaigns and social unrest. The speed with which deepfake content can go viral on social media platforms amplifies the potential damage, as false narratives can spread globally within hours. This has significant implications for national security, with the ability to destabilize governments, influence elections, and sway public opinion.

In response to the growing threat of deepfakes, AI-driven solutions are being developed to detect and mitigate these risks. Advanced machine learning models are now capable of identifying inconsistencies in deepfake videos, such as unnatural facial movements, inconsistent lighting, and unusual audio patterns. These detection tools analyze vast datasets of known real and fake content to learn patterns and behaviors specific to deepfakes, enabling them to spot new threats with high accuracy. However, as deepfake technology continues to evolve, so too must the detection methods, creating an ongoing arms race between malicious actors and cybersecurity professionals.

For organizations, defending against deep-fake threats requires a multi-layered security approach. It starts with awareness and education, ensuring that employees, clients, and stakeholders understand the risks associated with AI-powered media. Organizations must also invest in digital forensics tools capable of verifying the authenticity of digital content, especially when it comes to high-stakes communications, such as financial transactions, public announcements, or legal agreements. Building a robust response plan for deepfake-related incidents is essential, as the ability to quickly debunk false content and mitigate the damage can help preserve an organization's reputation and prevent financial losses.

Furthermore, governments and technology companies must collaborate to create policies and standards that address the ethical use of AI and deepfake technology. International agreements on the regulation of AI-powered threats, such as deep fakes, are necessary to create a unified response to this growing security concern. Public and private sectors must work together to create a secure digital environment where AI technologies are used responsibly, and malicious actors are held accountable for their actions.

AI and deepfake technologies represent a formidable challenge to digital security, creating new vulnerabilities and opportunities for cybercrime. As the line between real and fabricated content becomes increasingly blurred, organizations must adopt advanced detection techniques, invest in digital forensics tools, and build proactive defense strategies. By staying ahead of these emerging threats and fostering a culture of awareness and resilience, organizations can safeguard their digital assets and maintain trust in an increasingly digital world.

B. Blockchain and Cryptographic Solutions in Cyber Investigations

Blockchain and cryptographic technologies have revolutionized the way we think about security and data integrity. As cybercrime becomes more sophisticated, the integration of these solutions into digital forensics and cyber investigations has proven to be essential in safeguarding the integrity of data and ensuring transparent, tamper-proof records.

Blockchain, with its decentralized ledger system, provides a secure method for recording transactions and events that cannot be altered retroactively. This feature makes it invaluable for cyber investigations, as it can be used to verify digital evidence, track digital assets, and ensure the authenticity of data during forensic analysis. Investigators can leverage blockchain to track the movement of digital currencies in cybercrime cases, such as ransomware attacks or illegal online transactions, providing clear, traceable evidence that can withstand scrutiny in court.

Cryptographic techniques, on the other hand, are foundational in protecting sensitive data and ensuring confidentiality. In cyber investigations, encryption allows investigators to securely access and analyze data without compromising its integrity. With the rise of encrypted communications and data storage, forensic experts must rely on advanced cryptographic methods to decrypt and analyze potentially incriminating evidence, ensuring that they can track cybercriminals without violating privacy laws or regulations. By combining blockchain and cryptography, forensic investigators can create a robust system for both protecting and analyzing digital evidence in a way that is transparent, secure, and legally sound.

Moreover, as blockchain and cryptographic solutions continue to evolve, they are providing new ways to manage the security of digital assets, making it harder for cybercriminals to manipulate or destroy crucial evidence. This technology not only helps with tracking digital footprints but also ensures that the evidence used in cyber investigations remains untainted, providing greater confidence in the results of forensic analysis and facilitating successful prosecutions. These tools are fast becoming indispensable in the field of digital forensics and will likely play a crucial role in shaping the future of cybercrime investigations.

C. The Future of Automated Cybercrime Investigation

The landscape of cybercrime investigations is undergoing a transformative shift, fueled by advancements in automation and artificial intelligence (AI). As cyber threats continue to evolve in complexity and scale, traditional investigative methods are proving to be insufficient in keeping pace. To combat this growing challenge, the future of cybercrime investigations is inevitably moving toward greater automation. By leveraging cutting-edge technologies, automated systems can significantly enhance the efficiency, accuracy, and scope of digital forensics, creating an entirely new paradigm for how cybercrime is detected, investigated, and mitigated.

At the heart of automated cybercrime investigations lies the use of AI and machine learning algorithms. These technologies enable the automation of routine, time-consuming tasks that would traditionally require human intervention, such as log analysis, threat detection, and the identification of anomalous behavior. Machine learning models, for example, can continuously analyze vast amounts of data from networks, servers, and endpoints in real time, identifying potential threats faster than any human could. By doing so, automated systems can alert investigators to suspicious activity before it escalates into a full-scale attack, allowing for swift intervention and containment.

The future of automated cybercrime investigations also involves enhanced data correlation and pattern recognition. AI-powered tools can sift through large, disparate datasets from various sources such as network traffic logs, social media activity, and financial transactions identifying connections and correlations that might otherwise go unnoticed. This capability is crucial for uncovering hidden patterns in cybercriminal behavior, such as coordinated attacks, phishing campaigns, and fraud schemes. With advanced data analytics, investigators can piece together complex digital footprints and construct a clearer picture of the perpetrators behind cybercrimes.

Moreover, automation enabling faster and more accurate digital evidence processing. AI tools can autonomously analyze and process digital evidence, from emails and chat logs to file systems and encrypted data, in a fraction of the time it would take a human investigator. Automated systems can quickly classify evidence, detect anomalies, and identify relevant data, making the investigative process much more efficient. This speed is critical in cases where time is of the essence, such as in active cyberattacks or in investigating crimes where evidence is at risk of being destroyed or tampered with.

One of the most exciting prospects for the future of automated cybercrime investigations is the integration of predictive analytics. By using historical data, AI systems can anticipate future cyber threats and predict potential attack vectors before they happen. Predictive models can help investigators identify vulnerabilities in systems and networks, allowing them to strengthen defenses proactively. Additionally, these models can forecast the behaviors of cybercriminals, helping law enforcement and cybersecurity professionals prepare for emerging threats and strategize accordingly.

However, while automation offers significant advantages, it is not without its challenges. One of the key obstacles is the need for ongoing refinement and training of AI models. As cybercriminals continually develop new techniques, AI systems must be regularly updated to adapt to these evolving threats. Moreover, automated systems must be designed with transparency and accountability in mind, ensuring that human investigators can understand and trust the decisions made by AI tools.

Furthermore, the growing reliance on automation raises concerns about the potential for AI systems to be misused by cybercriminals. As automated tools become more powerful, so too does the potential for bad actors to exploit them for malicious purposes. For example, cybercriminals could use automated systems to launch large-scale attacks, bypass security protocols, or cover their tracks by erasing digital evidence. This highlights the need for robust safeguards and ethical considerations when developing and deploying automated investigation tools.

Despite these challenges, the future of automated cybercrime investigations holds tremendous promise. By enhancing the speed, accuracy, and efficiency of digital forensics, automation can help investigators stay ahead of cybercriminals, responding to threats in real time and minimizing damage. The integration of AI, machine learning, predictive analytics, and automated evidence processing will fundamentally change how cybercrime is investigated, enabling organizations and law enforcement agencies to fight back more effectively against the growing tide of cyber threats. As this field evolves, the role of human expertise will remain crucial, but the power of automation will serve as a critical ally in the battle against cybercrime.

CHAPTER NINE

Case Studies in AI-Driven Cyber Forensics

Artificial Intelligence (AI) has revolutionized digital forensics, providing cybersecurity professionals with powerful tools for investigating and mitigating cybercrime. This chapter examines several real-world case studies where AI-driven techniques have been successfully applied in cyber forensics. By exploring these cases, we gain a deeper understanding of the practical applications of AI in enhancing forensic investigations and improving overall cybersecurity resilience.

One prominent example of AI-driven cyber forensics is its role in combating ransomware attacks. In one case, a healthcare organization faced a sophisticated ransomware attack that encrypted critical patient data. Traditional forensic methods struggled to pinpoint the attack's origin and trace the ransomware's evolution. However, using AI-powered anomaly detection systems, investigators were able to identify unusual network behavior and isolate the attack's entry point. AI models also helped trace the ransomware's encrypted payload, ultimately leading to the recovery of vital data. This case demonstrated how AI's ability to rapidly analyze large volumes of data and detect anomalies can provide an invaluable edge in the fast-paced world of cybercrime investigations.

Another case study involves AI's integration with digital evidence processing in a large-scale financial fraud investigation. In this scenario, AI algorithms were used to automate the analysis of millions of transactional records, identifying suspicious patterns and anomalies in financial transactions. AI-driven predictive analytics were employed to uncover hidden connections between fraudulent accounts, helping investigators piece together a complex network of cybercriminal activities. The ability of AI to sift through vast datasets quickly and accurately helped expedite the investigation, enabling investigators to uncover fraud schemes that would have been nearly impossible to detect using traditional methods.

AI has also proven invaluable in combating insider threats, particularly within corporate environments. In one case, a financial services firm utilized AI-driven forensics to track unauthorized access to sensitive customer data. By analyzing patterns of user behavior, AI systems flagged suspicious activities that indicated a potential insider threat. Advanced machine learning models were used to build a profile of normal user behavior, making it easier to detect deviations from the norm. When an employee's account was identified as accessing sensitive data without proper authorization, AI-driven investigative tools helped trace the data's path and prevent further breaches. The case underscored the growing role of AI in detecting and mitigating insider threats before they escalate.

AI-powered digital forensics is also transforming investigations into the realm of intellectual property theft. In a case where a multinational corporation suspected that proprietary designs were being stolen by a competitor, AI algorithms were applied to monitor and analyze patterns of data access. The system's machine learning capabilities enabled investigators to identify the specific individuals responsible for downloading and transferring intellectual property. By integrating AI's ability to analyze network traffic and cross-reference digital footprints, investigators were able to track the data leak in real-time, leading to the recovery of stolen intellectual property and the identification of the perpetrators.

In these case studies, AI has proven to be a game-changer in digital forensics. Its ability to process vast amounts of data, detect hidden patterns, and predict potential threats has made it an essential tool for modern cybercrime investigations. AI-driven techniques not only enhance the efficiency of investigations but also provide higher accuracy and precision in identifying cybercriminal activities. As these technologies continue to evolve, they will undoubtedly play an even larger role in shaping the future of cybersecurity and digital forensics.

The integration of AI into cyber forensics represents a paradigm shift in how digital crimes are investigated and prosecuted. As we look forward to more complex cyber threats and increasingly sophisticated attackers, AI offers the necessary tools to stay ahead of the curve, ensuring that forensic professionals have the best resources available to combat cybercrime and safeguard digital ecosystems. These case studies highlight the practical advantages of AI and underscore its potential to significantly enhance the capabilities of digital forensics in the fight against cybercrime.

A. Notable Cybercrime Investigations and AI's Role

Cybercrime investigations are evolving, and artificial intelligence (AI) is playing an increasingly crucial role in transforming the way these cases are handled. Traditional methods of investigation often relied heavily on human expertise, manual analysis, and time-consuming processes. However, as cybercrimes grow in complexity and scale, AI technologies have become indispensable tools for law enforcement, forensic analysts, and cybersecurity professionals. By automating tedious tasks, identifying patterns, and enhancing investigative accuracy, AI is enabling faster, more effective responses to digital crimes.

One of the most notable examples of AI's role in cybercrime investigations comes from the field of malware detection. As ransomware and other malicious software evolve, human investigators struggle to keep up with the sheer volume and complexity of new strains. AI-based malware analysis tools, such as those using machine learning models, can quickly identify characteristics of new malware based on patterns learned from vast datasets. These systems can detect malicious activity with remarkable accuracy, even if the malware has never been encountered before. By flagging suspicious files or behavior, AI-powered tools assist investigators in isolating potential threats early in the attack lifecycle, allowing them to mitigate risks before significant damage occurs.

AI has also been pivotal in tackling financial cybercrime, such as money laundering and fraudulent transactions. Advanced AI systems can analyze financial networks and identify patterns indicative of illegal activity. In 2020, the use of AI helped identify a major global money laundering scheme, where vast amounts of illicit funds were being funneled through a network of shell companies. By examining transaction records, cross-referencing data points, and detecting inconsistencies, AI tools flagged suspicious transactions that were missed by traditional methods. This led to the uncovering of a complex, multi-layered fraud operation, resulting in the recovery of millions of dollars.

In addition to financial cybercrimes, AI has played a significant role in the investigation of cyber espionage cases. One such case involved a series of high-profile hacking incidents targeting government agencies and private corporations in the United States. AI-powered systems were instrumental in tracking the digital footprints of suspected state-sponsored hackers, uncovering how they infiltrated systems, exfiltrated sensitive data, and covered their tracks. AI-driven tools were able to analyze large amounts of communication logs, network traffic, and server records to identify patterns in the attackers' behaviors. By doing so, they helped cybersecurity professionals trace the attackers' movements across digital spaces, eventually leading to the attribution of the attacks to a specific foreign nation-state.

Another notable example is the rise in AI's use for social engineering attacks, particularly in the realm of phishing. AI algorithms now have the ability to mimic human behavior with frightening accuracy, generating emails and messages that are virtually indistinguishable from legitimate communications. In 2019, a sophisticated phishing campaign used AI-generated emails to impersonate high-ranking executives in major corporations, tricking employees into transferring sensitive company data. AI was used to automatically analyze social media profiles, email communication, and organizational structures to craft the most convincing impersonations. However, AI also helped investigators reverse-engineer the campaign by analyzing the patterns in the emails, identifying common traits, and flagging suspicious accounts. This analysis led to the arrest of several individuals involved in the operation, marking a milestone in the fight against AI-assisted cybercrime.

AI's application in cybercrime investigations is not limited to analyzing data; it is also being used to predict and prevent crimes before they occur. In predictive cybersecurity, AI-driven models analyze vast amounts of historical data to identify potential attack vectors and criminal behavior patterns. By recognizing these early warning signs, AI tools can alert cybersecurity teams to potential threats before they escalate. For example, AI models that track network traffic anomalies can proactively block an attacker's access to critical systems, preventing a data breach or other cybercrime before it happens. In this way, AI not only reacts to cybercrime but also serves as a powerful tool for prevention.

Despite its immense potential, AI is not without its challenges. One significant issue is the ability of cybercriminals to exploit AI for malicious purposes. Hackers are increasingly using AI to craft more sophisticated attacks, making it harder for traditional defenses to keep up. For instance, AI can be used to develop deep-fake videos and audio, which can be used for disinformation campaigns, extortion, or even identity theft. The very tools that are revolutionizing cybercrime investigations are also being adapted by cybercriminals to stay one step ahead. As a result, investigators and cybersecurity experts must constantly refine their AI systems, ensuring they evolve in tandem with the ever-changing cyber threat landscape.

AI's role in cybercrime investigations has already proven to be transformative, enabling more rapid and effective responses to a broad range of cyber threats. Its ability to process vast amounts of data, detect patterns, predict future threats, and enhance investigative accuracy has made it an invaluable asset in the fight against cybercrime. As technology continues to advance, AI will only become more integral to digital security, pushing the boundaries of what is possible in the investigation and prevention of cybercrime. The future of cybercrime investigations is undoubtedly tied to the capabilities of AI, and as we continue to innovate, its role in defending against digital threats will grow even more prominent.

B. Lessons Learned from High-Profile Digital Forensics Cases

The landscape of digital forensics is continually evolving as high-profile cybercrimes become more sophisticated and impactful. By analyzing past cases, investigators, cybersecurity professionals, and law enforcement agencies can gain invaluable insights into how to better approach digital forensics and enhance their ability to respond to future cyber threats. The lessons learned from these cases not only shed light on the critical role of forensic investigators but also highlight the importance of adapting to new technologies, strategies, and frameworks to ensure effective responses in an ever-changing digital world.

One key takeaway from high-profile digital forensics cases is the significance of early detection. In many cases, the delay in recognizing a cybercrime or breach led to severe consequences, including financial losses, compromised sensitive data, and long-lasting reputational damage. A notable example is the massive data breach of a global retail giant, which exposed the personal and financial information of millions of customers. The breach went undetected for several months, during which time the attackers exfiltrated sensitive data and exploited the vulnerabilities in the company's network. The case demonstrated that early detection and continuous monitoring are crucial for minimizing the damage caused by cybercriminals. Leveraging AI-driven tools and machine learning models for real-time threat detection can drastically improve an organization's ability to spot cybercrime early and take swift action to prevent further damage.

Another valuable lesson learned from high-profile cases is the necessity of preserving the integrity of digital evidence. In several high-profile cybercrime investigations, mishandling or improper collection of evidence led to critical data being compromised or excluded from the investigation. A well-documented and methodical process for digital evidence collection is essential to ensure that evidence remains admissible in court and can withstand legal scrutiny. In one case, a law enforcement agency's investigation into a hacker group was delayed due to the improper collection of digital evidence from seized devices. The incident highlighted the importance of using established forensic tools and maintaining a strict chain of custody to preserve the integrity of evidence from the initial collection point through to analysis and eventual court presentation.

High-profile cybercrime cases also underscore the need for multi-disciplinary collaboration. Investigations often require a diverse team of experts, including forensic analysts, cybersecurity professionals, legal specialists, and even public relations teams, all working in coordination. In one case involving the theft of intellectual property, a multinational company faced a sophisticated cyber-attack that required coordination between private forensic firms, government agencies, and law enforcement across multiple jurisdictions. The investigation took months to complete due to the international scope of the crime. The lesson learned here was that successful cybercrime investigations increasingly require a collaborative, cross-disciplinary approach, where experts from different fields contribute their specialized knowledge to the case.

Another critical lesson is the importance of having a proactive security posture. In many high-profile cases, organizations were unable to prevent cyber-attacks due to gaps in their security frameworks or outdated technology. A prime example is the WannaCry ransomware attack, which spread rapidly across organizations worldwide, causing widespread damage. The attack exploited known vulnerabilities that could have been patched with timely updates and security measures. This case illustrated the need for businesses and organizations to adopt a proactive approach to cybersecurity, ensuring that they stay up to date with the latest patches, conduct regular security assessments, and implement strong preventative measures to defend against emerging threats. An active threat-hunting program, coupled with continuous risk assessments, is crucial for identifying and addressing vulnerabilities before cybercriminals can exploit them.

The evolving nature of cybercrime also teaches that traditional forensic methods must be adapted to keep up with new technological advancements. In the case of a sophisticated cyber-espionage campaign that targeted government agencies, investigators struggled to trace the attackers due to the use of encryption, anonymous networks, and advanced malware. While traditional forensic methods were helpful in identifying some of the malicious code, they were not sufficient on their own to pinpoint the perpetrators. This highlighted the importance of integrating cutting-edge technologies like AI, machine learning, and blockchain forensics into traditional forensic processes. Modern cybercriminals are using increasingly sophisticated tools, and forensic professionals must continually adapt their techniques to stay ahead.

Finally, high-profile digital forensics cases reinforce the need for proper legal frameworks and international cooperation. Cybercrime is often transnational, with perpetrators operating across borders. In one prominent case, investigators faced significant challenges in accessing data stored on foreign servers, which delayed the investigation and hindered efforts to bring the criminals to justice. As cybercrime continues to grow in scope and complexity, collaboration between nations and the establishment of clear legal frameworks for international data access will be essential for ensuring that digital forensics can be effective in prosecuting cybercriminals.

The lessons learned from high-profile digital forensics cases emphasize the importance of vigilance, adaptability, collaboration, and proactive security measures. As cyber threats continue to evolve, it is critical for organizations and forensic professionals to adopt advanced technologies, update their processes, and refine their skills to stay ahead of cybercriminals. By applying the lessons from past cases, the cybersecurity industry can continue to improve its methods and resilience, ensuring that the fight against cybercrime remains effective and ever evolving.

C. Ethical Hacking and Cybersecurity Operations

In the ever-evolving landscape of digital threats, ethical hacking has emerged as a critical component in enhancing cybersecurity operations. Also known as penetration testing or white-hat hacking, ethical hacking involves legally and systematically testing systems, networks, and applications for vulnerabilities that malicious hackers might exploit. Unlike cybercriminals who aim to cause harm, ethical hackers work with organizations to identify weaknesses before they can be exploited, thereby strengthening security measures and ensuring the resilience of digital infrastructures.

Ethical hackers simulate real-world cyberattacks to uncover vulnerabilities within an organization's security framework. They use the same techniques and tools that black-hat hackers do, but with the permission of the organization to test. This proactive approach allows organizations to pinpoint weaknesses in their systems, applications, and networks, which can then be addressed before a real attack occurs. The goal is not just to discover vulnerabilities but also to understand how cybercriminals could exploit them, providing organizations with a comprehensive understanding of their security posture.

One of the key benefits of ethical hacking is that it provides an organization's cybersecurity team with actionable insights into potential risks. For example, an ethical hacker might identify a flaw in an authentication system that could be exploited to gain unauthorized access to sensitive data. By reporting this vulnerability, the ethical hacker allows the organization to patch the issue before it becomes a vector for a more sophisticated attack. The information provided by ethical hackers helps security teams improve their defenses, update their response protocols, and fortify their digital assets.

Ethical hackers also test the effectiveness of an organization's security policies, procedures, and controls. For instance, they may evaluate the adequacy of encryption standards or the robustness of network firewalls in defending against sophisticated attacks. These tests allow organizations to understand their weaknesses in a real-world context, rather than relying solely on theoretical analysis or automated tools. Ethical hacking also provides an opportunity to assess how well an organization's employees adhere to security protocols, such as recognizing phishing attempts or practicing proper password management.

The increasing sophistication of cyber threats has led to the integration of ethical hacking into mainstream cybersecurity operations. In large enterprises and government agencies, ethical hacking is now a crucial part of regular security audits and risk assessments. Cybersecurity operations that incorporate ethical hacking are often more resilient because they are continuously tested for vulnerabilities, and their security strategies are refined accordingly. These organizations are also better prepared to handle potential breaches and incidents since they are already familiar with the tactic cybercriminals may use.

Furthermore, ethical hackers contribute to cybersecurity operations by staying ahead of emerging trends and tactics used by cybercriminals. For example, with the rise of artificial intelligence (AI) and machine learning (ML) in cybersecurity, ethical hackers also employ these technologies to uncover hidden vulnerabilities or detect abnormal behavior within systems. They test for AI-driven attack vectors and help organizations understand how new technologies may be exploited by attackers. Ethical hacking operations are often iterative, with hackers continually re-evaluating an organization's security posture to address the changing threat landscape.

Collaboration between ethical hackers and cybersecurity teams also promotes a culture of continuous improvement in security operations. Ethical hackers provide critical feedback on existing security measures, helping teams identify not only technical flaws but also gaps in their security policies and practices. This feedback loop is invaluable, as it encourages proactive decision-making and quick adaptation to the constantly changing threat environment. The result is an organization's ability to remain one step ahead of adversaries and reduce the potential impact of cyberattacks.

In addition to organizational benefits, ethical hacking plays a pivotal role in protecting sensitive data and maintaining consumer trust. As more businesses move toward digital platforms, they accumulate vast amounts of sensitive information, such as customer data, financial records, and intellectual property. A breach of this data can lead to devastating consequences, both in terms of financial losses and reputational damage. Ethical hacking helps prevent these risks by identifying vulnerabilities that, if left unchecked, could result in unauthorized access to critical information. By strengthening security measures through ethical hacking, organizations not only protect themselves but also safeguard their customers' trust.

Moreover, ethical hacking is an essential tool for regulatory compliance. Many industries, such as healthcare, finance, and retail, are subject to stringent cybersecurity regulations and standards. Ethical hacking can help organizations demonstrate compliance by conducting tests and audits that ensure their systems meet the required security criteria. For example, ethical hackers might conduct penetration testing to validate that an organization adheres to the Payment Card Industry Data Security Standard (PCI DSS) or the General Data Protection Regulation (GDPR), ensuring that the organization is legally compliant and minimizing the risk of penalties.

The evolving nature of cyber threats means that ethical hacking will continue to play an integral role in cybersecurity operations. As attackers develop more sophisticated tactics, ethical hackers will need to adapt, leveraging new tools, technologies, and techniques to stay ahead. This ongoing adaptation will keep ethical hacking at the forefront of cybersecurity efforts, ensuring that organizations are always prepared to counter emerging threats and continue to operate securely in an increasingly digital world.

Ethical hacking is not just a preventive measure; it is an essential aspect of a proactive cybersecurity strategy. By identifying vulnerabilities, testing security protocols, and simulating real-world attacks, ethical hackers play a vital role in strengthening cybersecurity defenses and improving the resilience of digital infrastructures. As cyber threats continue to evolve, the collaboration between ethical hackers and cybersecurity professionals will remain a key factor in maintaining robust, secure systems for businesses and organizations worldwide.

CHAPTER TEN

The Road Ahead Strengthening Digital Security with AI

As cyber threats become increasingly sophisticated, the role of artificial intelligence (AI) in strengthening digital security has never been more critical. The fusion of AI and cybersecurity has ushered in a new era of threat detection, response, and mitigation, enabling organizations to defend themselves against cybercriminals with greater speed, accuracy, and foresight. The future of digital security is undeniably intertwined with the ongoing development of AI technologies, and this chapter explores how AI will continue to shape the trajectory of cybersecurity in the years to come.

AI's integration into digital security is poised to transform traditional cybersecurity practices by offering real-time, data-driven insights that are far more proactive and adaptive than manual interventions. The increasing complexity and volume of cyber threats make it impractical for human analysts to keep up, especially when relying on conventional methods. AI-powered systems, on the other hand, can process vast amounts of data in real-time, detect patterns, and identify anomalies that would otherwise go unnoticed. These capabilities not only enhance threat detection but also streamline the overall security response, significantly reducing the time between identifying a threat and neutralizing it.

One of the most promising applications of AI in digital security is its role in predictive threat intelligence. By analyzing historical attack data and current threat landscapes, AI systems can forecast potential security breaches, allowing organizations to preemptively strengthen their defenses. Machine learning (ML) models, a subset of AI, can be trained to detect evolving attack patterns, whether from known threats or zero-day vulnerabilities, and provide early warnings to security teams. This foresight enables businesses to make informed decisions, prioritize security measures, and allocate resources more effectively, ensuring that they are not merely reacting to cyber threats but anticipating them.

AI-driven automation is also revolutionizing how digital security incidents are handled. Automated systems equipped with machine learning algorithms can quickly assess the severity of an incident and take immediate action, such as isolating affected systems, blocking malicious traffic, or initiating a system-wide investigation. This real-time response, often in milliseconds, is crucial for mitigating the damage caused by attacks such as ransomware, data breaches, and denial-of-service (DoS) attacks. Automation also frees up human security analysts to focus on more complex issues, reducing their workload and allowing them to handle higher-level threats that require strategic thinking and expertise.

However, as AI continues to enhance digital security, it also brings with it new challenges. The same technologies that bolster defense mechanisms can be exploited by malicious actors. For example, cybercriminals may use AI to conduct more sophisticated attacks, such as AI-powered malware that adapts to security protocols, making it harder to detect. This raises the stakes for cybersecurity professionals, who must now develop countermeasures that not only combat traditional cyber threats but also guard against the very AI systems that criminals may employ. The race to outsmart attackers using

AI is an ongoing challenge, demanding continuous innovation and vigilance.

Another critical development in AI-powered digital security is its potential to improve the accuracy and efficiency of digital forensics. AI algorithms can be used to sift through massive volumes of digital evidence and identify patterns, behaviors, and links that might otherwise take investigators weeks or even months to uncover. Whether it's analyzing network traffic, reviewing server logs, or tracking user behavior, AI can accelerate the forensic investigation process, enabling faster response times in the aftermath of a cyberattack. The ability to efficiently process and analyze data also enhances the overall quality of digital evidence, which is crucial for successful legal proceedings and mitigating future security risks.

AI is also transforming the way organizations approach vulnerability management. Traditionally, identifying and patching security vulnerabilities involved manual scans and periodic updates. With AI, however, vulnerability detection has become more intelligent and dynamic. AI systems can continuously monitor an organization's digital infrastructure for vulnerabilities, predict where new weaknesses might emerge, and recommend patches or other mitigation strategies based on real-time data. This approach ensures that security gaps are addressed proactively, reducing the window of opportunity for cybercriminals to exploit them.

As AI technologies continue to evolve, the way we think about cybersecurity will undergo a fundamental shift. The emphasis will move from traditional, reactive security measures to more dynamic, anticipatory strategies that rely on the power of AI to predict, prevent, and respond to threats. In this future landscape, cybersecurity will be less about responding to incidents after they occur and more about creating an intelligent, resilient defense that can detect and neutralize threats before they have the chance to cause significant damage.

The integration of AI into digital security is also expanding into the realm of autonomous cybersecurity. In the future, it is not far-fetched to imagine a world where AI systems can autonomously detect and neutralize threats without human intervention. These AI-powered systems could operate 24/7, continuously analyzing data, identifying risks, and mitigating threats without the need for constant oversight. This level of automation would significantly improve efficiency, reduce the chances of human error, and allow organizations to focus their resources on more strategic and high-priority tasks.

While the potential of AI in digital security is immense, it is essential to recognize the importance of human oversight. AI systems are not infallible and must be monitored to ensure that they are functioning correctly and ethically. Human cybersecurity professionals will continue to play a crucial role in interpreting the insights provided by AI, making decisions on how to respond to potential threats, and ensuring that AI tools are used responsibly. The future of digital security will be a collaborative effort, where human expertise and AI technologies work in tandem to create a safer digital environment.

Looking forward, the road ahead for digital security is one where AI plays an increasingly central role in shaping the defenses of organizations worldwide. As cyber threats become more advanced, the need for intelligent, autonomous, and adaptive security solutions will be paramount. AI's ability to analyze vast amounts of data, predict future threats, and automate security processes will be critical in staying one step ahead of cybercriminals. The future of digital security is a landscape where AI not only enhances security protocols but revolutionizes the entire approach to cybersecurity, making it more resilient, agile, and proactive than ever before.

Ultimately, the combination of human ingenuity and AI's unparalleled computational power will ensure that organizations can defend themselves against the most sophisticated and persistent cyber threats. As we continue to navigate this rapidly evolving digital world, AI will remain a cornerstone of modern cybersecurity, safeguarding critical infrastructure, data, and privacy for generations to come.

A. The Role of Cybersecurity Professionals in AI-Enhanced Forensics

As the integration of artificial intelligence (AI) continues to redefine the landscape of cybersecurity, the role of cybersecurity professionals in AI-enhanced forensics becomes more critical than ever. These professionals are at the forefront of harnessing AI's capabilities to enhance the effectiveness and efficiency of digital investigations. Their expertise is essential in ensuring that AI tools are correctly applied to uncover cybercriminal activities, manage risks, and secure digital infrastructures.

Cybersecurity professionals play a pivotal role in integrating AI-driven solutions into existing forensic frameworks. Their understanding of both cybersecurity threats and forensic investigation protocols allows them to effectively incorporate AI technologies into the investigative process. AI-enhanced forensics can significantly speed up the identification of digital evidence and improve the accuracy of threat detection, but without cybersecurity professionals guiding the application of these technologies, organizations risk misinterpreting data or overlooking critical information. For instance, cybersecurity experts help fine-tune machine learning models to identify specific threat patterns, ensuring that AI systems are tailored to meet the unique needs of each investigation.

Moreover, cybersecurity professionals act as the bridge between AI systems and human analysis. While AI excels at processing vast amounts of data, it still requires human oversight for interpreting complex, context-dependent evidence. Cybersecurity experts are responsible for reviewing and validating the results provided by AI systems, ensuring that conclusions are accurate, relevant, and legally sound. This collaboration between human expertise and AI's analytical power creates a more robust forensic investigation process, where AI can quickly flag potential threats and provide insights, while professionals can use their judgment to make informed decisions on the next steps in the investigation.

The application of AI in cyber forensics also presents unique challenges in terms of data privacy and ethics. Cybersecurity professionals must navigate these complexities, ensuring that AI tools are used in compliance with privacy laws and ethical guidelines. The use of AI in surveillance and data analysis, particularly in high-stakes criminal investigations, raises concerns about data security, unauthorized access, and biases in algorithmic decision-making. It is the responsibility of cybersecurity professionals to ensure that AI applications are transparent, equitable, and accountable. They must also ensure that data handling and processing procedures uphold the integrity of digital evidence, ensuring that it can be used in legal proceedings without compromising the privacy of individuals or organizations.

Additionally, as AI continues to evolve, cybersecurity professionals are instrumental in keeping up with advancements and ensuring that AI tools remain effective against emerging cyber threats. The rapid development of AI technologies means that cybersecurity experts must stay ahead of the curve, constantly learning and adapting to new capabilities in AI-driven forensics. They must understand how AI models are trained, how they process information, and how they can be exploited by cybercriminals. By staying abreast of the latest trends in AI and machine learning, cybersecurity professionals can help refine forensic methodologies and implement new strategies to combat increasingly sophisticated cybercrime.

Another key responsibility of cybersecurity professionals is ensuring the scalability of AI-enhanced forensics. As organizations grow and their digital infrastructures become more complex, the volume of data generated increases exponentially. AI tools must be designed to scale effectively, capable of handling large datasets and identifying threats in real time across diverse environments. Cybersecurity professionals are responsible for deploying and managing AI solutions that can handle this data load, ensuring that organizations can maintain their security posture as they expand.

Finally, cybersecurity professionals act as educators and mentors in the field of AI-enhanced forensics. As AI technologies become more prevalent, the demand for skilled professionals who can operate and manage these tools is increasing. Cybersecurity experts are in a unique position to educate the next generation of forensic analysts, helping them understand the fundamentals of AI and how to incorporate these techniques into their investigative practices. They can also provide guidance to other sectors, such as law enforcement and government agencies, on how AI-driven tools can be used to enhance cybercrime investigations and improve overall security practices.

The role of cybersecurity professionals in AI-enhanced forensics is multi-faceted and indispensable. From overseeing the implementation of AI tools to ensuring data privacy, scalability, and ethical standards, cybersecurity experts provide the necessary human expertise to complement AI's analytical capabilities. As AI continues to revolutionize cyber forensics, these professionals will be instrumental in shaping the future of digital investigations, driving innovation, and ensuring that AI's potential is fully realized in the fight against cybercrime.

B. Policy and Governance for AI in Cybersecurity

The rapid advancement of artificial intelligence (AI) has profoundly impacted the cybersecurity landscape, offering new opportunities to enhance threat detection, automate responses, and bolster digital resilience. However, as AI technologies become integral to cybersecurity strategies, the need for robust policy frameworks and governance mechanisms becomes critical. Ensuring the ethical and responsible use of AI in cybersecurity is essential not only to safeguard sensitive data but also to maintain trust in digital systems and technologies.

Establishing Comprehensive AI Governance Models

The integration of AI into cybersecurity operations introduces complexities that require a cohesive governance structure. These frameworks need to address several key areas: ethical guidelines, accountability, transparency, data privacy, and regulatory compliance. Cybersecurity policies must be established to guide the development, deployment, and monitoring of AI tools, ensuring they align with legal standards and ethical norms. Governance models should also consider the potential for bias in AI algorithms, establishing protocols for fairness and objectivity in automated decision-making. For example, cybersecurity systems using AI for threat detection must be governed to ensure they do not unfairly target specific groups or systems, thus preserving the integrity and trustworthiness of the AI systems in place.

A well-defined policy for AI governance in cybersecurity should include clear roles and responsibilities for oversight, risk management, and continuous monitoring. This includes defining who is responsible for ensuring AI algorithms are trained and maintained correctly, as well as implementing measures to track the performance and effectiveness of AI systems in real-time. Effective governance structures will involve stakeholders from a variety of departments, including IT, legal, compliance, and data privacy, to ensure a holistic approach to AI's role in cybersecurity.

Ethical and Regulatory Compliance in AI Systems

AI-driven cybersecurity tools have the potential to collect, analyze, and process vast amounts of data, much of which may be sensitive. As such, policies surrounding data privacy, ownership, and protection must be enforced rigorously. Organizations need to implement AI systems that respect data protection regulations such as the General Data Protection Regulation (GDPR), Health Insurance Portability and Accountability Act (HIPAA), and other jurisdiction-specific laws governing digital data privacy. A well-developed policy will ensure that AI tools used for threat detection and response do not inadvertently violate data privacy rights or overstep ethical boundaries.

Moreover, AI's role in cybersecurity raises critical questions about accountability, particularly when automated systems make decisions about threats or vulnerabilities. Governance frameworks must address who is ultimately responsible for AI-driven actions, especially in situations where an AI system makes a false positive or false negative regarding an alleged threat. Clear accountability measures must be implemented to ensure that organizations can trace the decision-making process of AI systems, providing a clear understanding of why certain actions were taken, and who should be held accountable in case of errors or unintended consequences.

Establishing Standards and Best Practices for AI in Cybersecurity

As AI technologies in cybersecurity continue to evolve, the establishment of industry standards and best practices becomes essential to guide organizations in implementing AI solutions safely and effectively. Governments, international organizations, and industry bodies are working together to set these standards, ensuring that AI is used consistently and reliably across different sectors. These standards can cover everything from AI algorithm development and training processes to guidelines on testing and validating AI systems before they are deployed in real-world environments. Developing global standards for AI applications in cybersecurity will enable better collaboration between governments, private sectors, and security professionals to manage and regulate the widespread adoption of AI technologies.

These standards can also help mitigate the risk of AI-driven tools being used maliciously by bad actors. Cybercriminals have begun to leverage AI to launch more sophisticated attacks, such as automated spear phishing or AI-powered malware. In response, cybersecurity professionals must ensure their AI systems are safeguarded against exploitation and adversarial attacks. Governance policies should include proactive threat intelligence, collaborative defense strategies, and the sharing of cybersecurity research to anticipate and neutralize emerging AI-based threats. This will help create a global defense network where all parties can benefit from shared information and improved standards.

Transparency, Trust, and Public Awareness

As AI continues to be integrated into cybersecurity systems, building public trust is critical. One of the primary concerns surrounding the use of AI in cybersecurity is the lack of transparency regarding how decisions are made by AI systems. Whether it's a matter of protecting personal privacy or mitigating cyber risks, organizations must clearly communicate how their AI tool's function and the underlying processes that inform their actions. Transparency helps foster trust among stakeholders, including consumers, regulatory bodies, and the general public.

Governments and organizations should work together to develop frameworks that require AI systems to be explainable and auditable. This means that decisions made by AI tools, such as flagging security incidents or blocking access to a system, should be traceable and understandable to human auditors. This level of transparency is crucial in cases where the use of AI could have significant legal, ethical, or financial ramifications. Policymakers must ensure that the public is educated on the role of AI in cybersecurity and the safeguards in place to protect their data and privacy. Public awareness initiatives can help demystify AI technologies, empowering individuals to understand how they work and the security measures that protect their interests.

Adapting to the Evolving Cybersecurity Landscape

As AI continues to transform the cybersecurity field, organizations must be agile enough to adapt to an ever-evolving threat landscape. This means not only adopting the latest AI tools but also ensuring that governance frameworks are flexible and capable of evolving alongside technological advancements. Policies and governance models must be regularly reviewed and updated to account for new AI capabilities, emerging risks, and changing regulatory requirements.

By fostering a forward-thinking approach to AI governance, organizations can better prepare for the complexities and challenges posed by AI in cybersecurity. Well-structured policies will support the responsible integration of AI technologies, allowing businesses and government agencies to enhance their digital security while maintaining the highest standards of governance, ethics, and compliance.

The importance of policy and governance for AI in cybersecurity cannot be overstated. As AI continues to revolutionize the cybersecurity space, ensuring ethical use, regulatory compliance, and public trust will be key to leveraging its full potential while mitigating risks. Robust governance structures will enable organizations to not only combat emerging threats more effectively but also set the groundwork for sustainable, responsible AI-driven cybersecurity.

C. Preparing for the Next Generation of Cyber Threats

As we stand on the brink of a new era in cybersecurity, the rapid advancement of technology presents both opportunities and challenges. The digital landscape is evolving at an unprecedented pace, with new innovations such as the Internet of Things (IoT), 5G connectivity, and artificial intelligence (AI) creating a more interconnected and complex environment. With these developments come new, more sophisticated cyber threats that are more difficult to predict, detect, and neutralize. The next generation of cyber threats will require a forward-thinking approach, one that combines the latest advancements in technology with proactive strategies and a deep understanding of emerging risks.

One of the key aspects of preparing for these future threats lies in the ability to anticipate where vulnerabilities might arise. Cybersecurity today must move beyond traditional defense mechanisms and focus on anticipating how adversaries will exploit new technologies. The rise of AI, for example, introduces the potential for AI-powered cyberattacks, where malicious actors could leverage machine learning and automation to develop more complex and adaptable threats. These types of attacks may be able to learn from previous breaches and modify their behavior to evade detection by traditional security measures. To combat this, cybersecurity professionals must develop AI-driven defense systems that are capable of outsmarting these advanced attacks in real-time.

As the digital landscape continues to expand, the attack surface for cybercriminals becomes increasingly vast. With billions of devices connected to the internet, from smart appliances to industrial machines, there are more potential entry points for attackers to exploit. This rapid growth in interconnected devices is making it crucial for organizations to develop more comprehensive security strategies that include not only traditional network security but also robust safeguards for IoT devices, edge computing systems, and cloud infrastructures. Security protocols will need to evolve to account for the unique vulnerabilities associated with each of these emerging technologies, ensuring that all components of a network are adequately protected from potential threats.

To prepare for these evolving threats, organizations must embrace a proactive cybersecurity posture, where risk management, threat detection, and incident response are built into the very foundation of their digital infrastructure. This means implementing continuous monitoring and real-time threat intelligence that can detect unusual activities and vulnerabilities before they can be exploited. AI and machine learning will play a pivotal role in this approach, with predictive models that can forecast potential cyberattacks based on data trends and emerging threat patterns. These intelligent systems will allow organizations to respond to threats in their infancy, reducing the likelihood of successful attacks and mitigating the damage that could occur.

Moreover, preparing for the next generation of cyber threats will require a shift in how cybersecurity professionals approach training, collaboration, and knowledge sharing. The cybersecurity workforce must be equipped with the latest skills and tools to handle advanced threats. This includes ongoing education in emerging technologies such as AI, blockchain, and quantum computing, as well as training in ethical hacking, digital forensics, and incident response. Cybersecurity teams must also work closely with other departments within an organization, ensuring that security is integrated into every aspect of the business. In this interconnected world, cybersecurity cannot be siloed but must be a collaborative effort that includes all stakeholders, from IT teams to executives.

Another key aspect of preparing for future cyber threats is strengthening the resilience of digital systems. Resilience refers to the ability of a system to continue functioning effectively even in the face of an attack or breach. This is particularly important as cybercriminals become more adept at launching multi-vector attacks, where they target not just one system but several interconnected components of an organization's infrastructure. Developing systems that are resilient to these types of attacks requires building redundancy into critical systems, having failover mechanisms in place, and ensuring that data is regularly backed up and protected from ransomware attacks. Additionally, organizations must implement a culture of cybersecurity awareness at all levels, ensuring that employees are trained to recognize and respond to potential threats quickly and effectively.

As the threat landscape evolves, the need for robust cybersecurity regulations and frameworks becomes increasingly important. Governments, regulatory bodies, and international organizations must collaborate to establish standards and best practices that guide organizations in safeguarding their digital infrastructures. These frameworks should address the specific risks posed by emerging technologies, set clear guidelines for protecting sensitive data, and provide a roadmap for responding to and recovering from cyberattacks. Additionally, governments must invest in advancing their own cybersecurity capabilities, as nation-state actors will continue to be a significant threat to both public and private sector organizations.

One of the most pressing challenges for the future of cybersecurity will be balancing the need for robust security measures with the increasing demand for privacy and data protection. As the digital world becomes more interconnected, organizations will have access to more data than ever before, which increases the risk of data breaches and privacy violations. Cybersecurity frameworks will need to evolve to not only protect against cyber threats but also ensure that data is handled in accordance with privacy laws and regulations. This will require greater collaboration between security and compliance teams, as well as the development of technologies that can protect personal information while still allowing for the advanced analysis needed to detect and prevent cybercrime.

Finally, the next generation of cybersecurity will rely on a shift from a reactive approach to a more proactive and anticipatory one. Traditional methods of defense, such as firewalls and antivirus software, are no longer sufficient in a world where cyberattacks are more advanced, targeted, and persistent. To stay ahead of cybercriminals, organizations must adopt a mindset of continuous improvement, constantly evolving their security protocols to stay one step ahead of emerging threats. This involves integrating advanced technologies like AI, machine learning, and blockchain into security infrastructures, developing more sophisticated threat detection and response strategies, and fostering a culture of collaboration and innovation across industries and sectors.

In the end, preparing for the next generation of cyber threats will require organizations to be adaptable, forward-thinking, and willing to invest in both the technologies and skills needed to combat increasingly complex threats. By staying ahead of the curve, fostering innovation, and embracing new technologies, businesses, governments, and individuals can create a more secure and resilient digital future. The journey ahead will undoubtedly be challenging, but with the right strategies, tools, and mindset, we can ensure that the digital world remains safe and secure for years to come.

www.ingramcontent.com/pod-product-compliance
Lightning Source LLC
LaVergne TN
LVHW101503200926
848483LV00001B/207